Mixtow

Mixtow limekiln, with Colvithick Wood behind, 1814.
(*Cornwall Record Office*)

Roger and Alexa

Mixtow

A History

Martin Sheppard

with best wishes

Mart Shppd

SCOTFORTH

First published in 2014 on behalf of the author by
Scotforth Books (www.scotforthbooks.com)
ISBN   978-1-909817-18-0
Typesetting and design by Carnegie Book Production, Lancaster.
Printed in the UK by Jellyfish Solutions

Contents

Illustrations

Text Illustrations

Acknowledgements

I am extremely grateful to the following for permission to reproduce illustrations: the British Library, 1; Sheila Cheadle, p. 94; the Cornwall Record Office, pp. 2, 24 and 25; Betty Davies, 22 and 23; Imerys, 28 and 29; Wendy Parfitt, 21; Isabel Pickering 12–14; John Pollard, 24; Paul Richards, 4, 5, 7–11, 16, 17; the Royal Fowey Yacht Club, 20; Hilary Severn, 27; Lucy Sheppard, 30 and 31; Samuel Sheppard, 3; Penny Tuck, 25 and 26; and Catherine Turbett, 32 and 33.

Introduction

M IXTOW IS OF little interest to the outside world. An unimportant farming and fishing community in the past, it is now shared between farmers, residents, second-home owners and holiday-makers. Since the building of the Lostwithiel and Fowey Railway in the 1860s, it has looked across to Fowey Docks, giving those at Mixtow a prime view of the boats loading there, as well as a panorama of the traffic, from dredgers and tugs to motor boats, gigs and canoes, using the river. Reflecting the modern popularity of sailing, in the summer Mixtow Pill is full of yachts.

That Mixtow has not been the scene of sensational events, if the distant echoes of piracy and smuggling are discounted, does not mean that it is without a history. It has been closely connected with the fortunes of Fowey, sharing its magnificent harbour, since the town's foundation. Close to the Iron Age citadel of Castle Dore, it was undoubtedly visited long ago by those using the river but leaving no trace (Tantalisingly, a Bronze Age sword was found during dredging near Mixtow Quay.)[1] There are records of Mixtow's manors and farms going back many hundreds of years, while the first Royal Navy chart of the harbour, showing Mixtow Pill, dates from the second half of the eighteenth century. Complete surveys of land holding, giving ownership in great detail, were compiled in the early 1840s and between 1910 and 1915. A more recent survey of crops and livestock was made during the Second World War. Books on local history, material in local and national archives, census and land tax returns, wills and conveyances, and reports in the local newspapers, as well as interviews with past and present inhabitants of Mixtow, supplement these records.

Immediately above Fowey on the river, Mixtow has no official identity, being only part of the parish of Lanteglos by Fowey. I have taken it as being Mixtow Pill itself, and the fields and houses on its banks, as well as those to either side of the pill. I have included the local farms, Castle, Dorset, Lombard, Mixtow and Yeate (as well as the more recent Polrose), whose fields stretch from Penpoll to Bodinnick; and the lanes running between Castle Farm and Whitecross; and from Lombard Farm towards Highway. The main channel of the River Fowey, as it passes Mixtow Pill, is also an integral part of Mixtow. This is reflected in my account of the development of the docks on the opposite bank of the river since the 1860s.

History can only be based on surviving records. By their nature, these tend to be official rather than unofficial. While I have tried to find out about the characters of those who lived and worked at Mixtow over the centuries, and to discover what they looked like, for the majority of these men, women and children this is impossible. Talking to those with long memories of Mixtow has, however, revealed far more personal detail than might otherwise have been the case.

Writing the history of Mixtow has been its own reward. I have been interested to see what can be discovered about a small and largely unexceptional rural area, trying to make sense of the changes to it over the centuries. In doing so, I am grateful for the help given to me by the staff of the Cornwall Record Office, the National Archives, the National Hydrographic Office and the Royal Institution of Cornwall. Derek Giles and Ivan Bowditch made my visit to the China Clay History Society Archive a pleasure. Isabel Pickering, the doyenne of Fowey history, very kindly sent me her notes on the history of Mixtow. Professor Caroline Barron, Dr Helen Doe and Sam Drake have helped in specific but most valuable ways. Piecing together the sequence of property transfers at Mixtow was only made possible by the willingness of Dave and Shirley Bieber, George Seppings and Penny Tuck to allow me to examine the title deeds to their properties. I am also grateful to Jennifer Burden and Jenna Sellars of Stephens Scown, for letting me to go through the deeds of Mixtow House in their offices in St Austell, and to Claire Bennett for sending me a list of the owners of Henwood. For modern times, the reminiscences of those who have lived at or been connected with Mixtow have proved invaluable. In particular, I would like to thank Madge Norman for telling me about the recent history of its farms. Isabel Pickering, John Pollard, Paul Richards, Hilary Severn and Penny Tuck all provided illustrations. Dave Bieber, Richard and Maggie Davies, Madge Norman, John Pollard, Henry Poole, Bob Saxton, Lucy Sheppard and Geoffrey Simpson kindly read my final chapter and saved me from many errors. Finally, I am greatly indebted to Lucy Frontani, Anna Goddard and Alistair Hodge of Carnegie Publishing for their expert advice and encouragement in the production of this book.

This small book is dedicated to Henry Poole, who suggested that I write it.

1

Lanteglos by Fowey

THE HISTORY OF MIXTOW, in the parish of Lanteglos by Fowey on the south coast of Cornwall, cannot easily be separated from that of Fowey; or from that of the other main settlements on the estuary of the River Fowey, Lostwithiel, Bodinnick and Polruan. Not on the road to anywhere, Mixtow's communications with its larger neighbours have always been as much by water as by land.[1]

The wide estuary of the River Fowey is one of a series of sunken valleys which mark the south coast of Devon and Cornwall. To its east are the Dart, the Tamar and the Looe; and to its west the Fal and the Helford rivers. The estuaries of all these provide excellent anchorages, which made them obvious sites for trade and settlement. The advantages of Plymouth's natural harbour were so great that it became one of the main bases of the Royal Navy.

The River Fowey, which rises above Dozmary Pool on Bodmin Moor, is fed on its way south west by a number of smaller streams. It also has a number of the substantial tidal creeks characteristic of the southern rivers of Cornwall. Lerryn, Penpoll Creek and Pont Creek are tidal estuaries in their own right, full at high water but muddy at low tide, stretching a mile or more from the main channel. Each is fed by its own rivulet, respectively the Lerryn river, Trebant water and Pont stream. There are two small creeks on the western bank: Woodgate Pill, north of

Golant, and Bodmin Creek.[2] Opposite Bodinnick, what was once a creek at the mouth of Caffa Mill stream has been filled in.*

The River Fowey has one other inlet, larger than Woodgate Pill but smaller than the three main creeks. Above Pont but below Penpoll lies Mixtow Pill. Fed by two local streams, there is less than four hundred yards from the main river to its furthest point at Merrifield. Like its larger neighbours, it is fully tidal. It makes a distinctive indentation in the river, with steep banks rising around it on all sides.

There is no doubt of the antiquity of the wider area around Mixtow in terms of habitation. On the west bank of the river above Golant is the striking Iron Age fort of Castle Dore, strategically placed to command the Fowey estuary and what was once a landing place at the mouth of the Luxulyan river. It has even been claimed that Castle Dore was the site of the palace of King Mark of Cornwall, the uncle of Tristan and the husband of Isolde.[3] A remarkable early stone, with a reference to Tristan, was found there.†

Fowey itself, on the west bank of the river, was a relative latecomer, as in medieval times it was overshadowed in importance by Lostwithiel, where a bridge has crossed the river since the twelfth century. That this bridge is still the first crossing of the river has undoubtedly had a major effect on the subsequent history of all the communities on its banks.‡ Plans for a bridge to replace the Bodinnick Ferry have never come to fruition; and Polruan, facing Fowey from the east at the harbour's mouth, is still only linked to Fowey by a passenger ferry.[4] Lostwithiel was also near the castle of Restormel, the centre of the lordship of Cornwall exercised

---

*   Initially, only part of it was filled in, as the site of a station. It is now one of Fowey's three main car parks.

†   The Tristan Stone, a weathered, seven-foot high stone dating from the fifth century, bears the inscription, 'Drustanus hic iacet Cunomori filius', which can be translated as 'Here lies Drustanus, son of Cunomorus'. Drustanus is a known variant of Tristan. The stone is currently on the roadside above Fowey, between Four Turnings and the New Road. Moved from near Castle Dore to its present site, it is currently threatened by a second move, to a nearby field, following the grant of planning permission to a developer, Wainhomes. *Daily Mail*, 13 December 2012.

‡   The bridge at Lostwithiel has been rebuilt several times. The current bridge is described by Nikolaus Pevsner, *Cornwall* (second edn, Harmondsworth, 1970), p. 107, as an 'early C14 bridge of five pointed arches with double rings to their voussoirs'. The bridge once extended further west towards the church, while its eastern extension dates only from the eighteenth century.

by Richard of Cornwall, the brother of Henry III, and other royal holders. It was the site of the main Stannary parliament, regulating tin mining, and had rights over trade on the river. By 1304 Lostwithiel was sending two members to Parliament. Its gradually dwindling importance was due to silting, partly from the excess waste material poured into the river by tin-miners.[5] The antiquary and traveller John Leland, writing during the reign of Henry VIII, expressed this graphically:

> The stone bridge in tyme of memorie of men lyving was of arches very depe to the sight, the sande is now cum to within four or five fote of the very hedde of them. The sande that cummith from tynne workes is a great cause of this: and yn tyme to cum shaul be a sore decay to the hole haven. Barges yet cum with martchanties with in half a mile of Lostwithiel.[6]

Lostwithiel's loss was Fowey's gain. It thrived, growing first to rival and then to eclipse the older port.[7] It was granted a charter by the prior of Tywardreath in the early thirteenth century, allowing it a sizeable measure of self-government.[8] Its quays were safer to use than the landing place at the mouth of the Luxulyan river, and its deep water allowed large vessels to moor and unload when they could no longer reach Lostwithiel. A narrow tangle of houses, warehouses, fish cellars and quays, medieval Fowey stretched from the north gate near the old landing place of the Bodinnick ferry to the south gate just beyond the church of St Fimbarrus, rebuilt magnificently in this period.[9] In early Tudor times, the town was described by the antiquary and traveller John Leland as 'set on the north side of the haven, and is set hanging on a maine rokky hille, and is in length about a quarter of a mile'.[10]

In the fourteenth and fifteenth centuries Fowey achieved a prominence that defied its modest size, benefiting rather than suffering from its remote location. Medieval sailors, wherever possible, preferred to hug the coast rather than to sail out of sight of land. Fowey was a familiar and welcome landfall to ships from the west of France, and from Spain, Portugal and the Mediterranean. Reflecting this, and its importance as a trading centre, Fowey's population of perhaps a thousand in this period included many foreigners.[11] Fowey was described by Leland as 'hauntid with shippes of diverse nations, and their shippes went to al nations'.[12] The alien subsidy of 1439 lists twenty-seven foreign householders in the port: nine from Ireland, five from Flanders, two from Brittany, and one each from Gascony and Portugal; and another twenty-nine non-house-holders mostly from the same places.[13]

By the mid fourteenth century Fowey had built up a substantial national and international trade, exporting cheese, cloth, hides, meat and pilchards, and bringing back wine, salt, metal goods and fruit from France and Spain.[14] Its ships also carried pilgrims to the shrine of St James of Compostela in north-west Spain. The most important trading commodity in this period was, however, undoubtedly tin.[15] These centuries also saw a peak in the local importance of tin mining, based primarily around Bodmin and Lostwithiel and employing perhaps three thousand men.[16] The value of the metal was reflected in the careful scrutiny of pieces of tin by the Stannary parliament at Lostwithiel, to ensure its full taxation, and in the links forged between London and Fowey at the time. Most tin was shipped in Fowey ships to London, after being brought down from Lostwithiel by barge. Tin was also shipped to Southampton for re-export or for carriage overland to London.

Although Cornwall is often thought of as having been remote from the rest of England, it is clear that London merchants were behind much of Fowey's trade.[17] It is also possible to identify Cornishmen of note in the medieval London. Even in the fifteenth century members of the Cornish gentry, sometimes with their families, seem to have ridden up to London with surprising frequency. The crown also took a considerable interest in Fowey, both because of the taxable value of tin and other duties, and because of its contribution to England's war effort. In times of war, Fowey's ships and seasoned sailors were regularly employed by the crown to transport men and stores to France, Ireland or Scotland.

The name Mixtow is undoubtedly an abbreviation of Michaelstow, meaning the church or holy place of St Michael.[*] It is possible that there was a chapel there once, dedicated to St Michael, but there is no evidence other than its name to support this. Mixtow is in the parish of Lanteglos by Fowey, which consists of around three thousand acres surrounded by

---

[*] St Michael is closely associated with Cornwall, most famously at St Michael's Mount. There is also a parish of Michaelstowe in north Cornwall, near Camelford. On Cornwall and its patron archangel and saint, see Henderson, *Essays in Cornish History* (Oxford, 1935), pp. 197–201. The parish of Lanteglos by Fowey must not be confused with that of Lanteglos by Camelford.

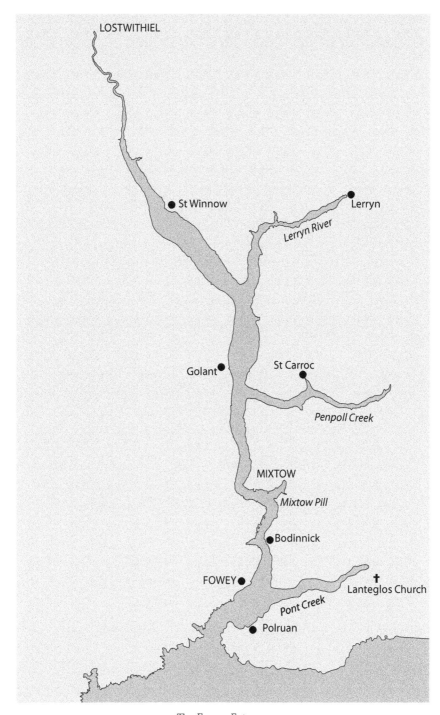

LOSTWITHIEL

St Winnow

Lerryn

Lerryn River

Golant

St Carroc

Penpoll Creek

MIXTOW

Mixtow Pill

Bodinnick

FOWEY

† Lanteglos Church

Pont Creek

Polruan

The Fowey Estuary

water on three sides: to the south the sea, to the west the River Fowey and
to the north Penpoll Creek. Its church, dedicated to the shadowy Irish
saint St Wyllow, is at the centre of the parish, above the end of Pont Creek
but away from its main settlements, Polruan and Bodinnick. The church's
position reflects the spread of farms throughout the parish: these were
established before either the fishing community at Polruan or the ferry at
Bodinnick. (A ferry at Bodinnick is known to have been in existence from
the fourteenth century, but one must have been in existence before then.)
St Wyllow has traces of an earlier Norman church but, in the fourteenth
century, was rebuilt handsomely, reflecting the patronage of the powerful
Mohun family of Bodinnick and the prosperity of Polruan.[18]

The first document relating explicitly to land at Mixtow (in the form
'Myghelstowe') is a release, dating from 1409 and confirming the rights
to a house and garden of Richard Martyn of Bodinnick. Two other houses,
one of each side of that belonging to Martyn, are also mentioned, with
the names of their owners. Where these houses were exactly is impossible
to know with any certainty. The release, however, confirms the antiquity
of the settlement at Mixtow.

I Stephen Bodulgate release and quit claim on behalf of myself and
my heirs to Richard Martyn of Bodennok all the right and claim that
I have in the tenement with attached garden and all appurtenances
in the town of Myghelstowe, situated between the tenement of Rose,
widow of Simon Boton, on one side and the tenement of Henry Legat
on the other side. And no right or legal claim to the said tenement and
garden and appurtenances in the aforesaid town will remain to me or
my heirs. I exclude myself forever from any right or claim to sell, or to
reclaim, the property.

In witness whereof I have placed my seal. Witnesses Thomas Mohun,
Thomas Treffry, Richard Stonard, John Lamelyn, Robert Mayhowe and
others.[19]

Dated at Myghelstowe Monday next after the feast of St Michael the
Archangel in the tenth[20] year of King Henry IV.*

* Courtney Library, Royal Institution of Cornwall, Truro, TAM/1/3/32/3. I am
extremely grateful to Professor Caroline Barron for translating this document from
the original Latin. The surname Mixtow appears earlier as that of Fowey's most

One of the earliest English antiquaries, William Worcestre, passed through Lanteglos in 1478, staying the night with a friend, Robert Bracey, at Bodinnick. Bracey told him about the life of St Wyllow, who was 'beheaded by Melyn ys Kynrede, near the place where Walter, bishop of Norwich, was born, and carried his head to St Wyllow's Bridge for half a mile to the spot where the said church was founded in his honour'.[21]

Besides the main church, there were a number of chapels in the parish. The remains of the chapel of St Saviour in Polruan, for which records go back to 1284 and which served as a landmark for sailors, can be seen from Mixtow.[22] A chapel dedicated to St John the Baptist in Bodinnick was licensed in 1406. There were also private chapels at Hall, above Bodinnick, recorded in 1374, and at Lanlawren.[23] Nearer to Mixtow, though separated from it by Penpoll Creek, is the site of one of Cornwall's few monastic houses. This was St Carroc, a cell of the Cluniac priory of Montacute in Somerset, dating from the second half of the twelfth century. Montacute owned land and other property in Cornwall and administered these from St Carroc. St Carroc was surrendered to Henry VIII's commissioners in March 1539, at the same time as Montacute. Although its chapel was still standing in the 1590s, there are now no visible traces of the monastic buildings.[24]

John Leland, on his itinerary in about 1540, after visiting Fowey and Lostwithiel, worked his way down the east bank of the River Fowey:

> From Lostwithiel doun along Fawey Ryver to St Winnous an abate chirch a good mile … By this chirch is a warfe to make shippes on … From St Guinows chirch to the point of St Winows Wood half a mile. Here goith yn a salt crek half a mile on the east side of the haven, and at the hed of it is a bridge caullid Lerine Bridge, and the creeke berith also the name of Lerine … From Lerine Creke to St Carac Pille or Creeke about half a mile lower on the said est side of the haven, it goith a mile …[25]

Finally, he reached Mixtow: 'From the moth of St Carak Pille to Poul-Morlande Pille about a mile, it goith scant a quarter of a mile up into

---

notorious medieval inhabitants in many forms, including Mexstowe, Michaelstow, Michelstow, Michelstowe, Michellstow, Mighelstow, Mighelestowe, Mighistow, Mikulstowe, Mistowe, Mixstowe, Mixtan, Mixto, Myghelstowe and Mykstowe. See Drake, 'Fowey during the Hundred Years' War', appendixes, pp. 12, 13, 22–24.

the lande: it at the hedde goith into two armes. From the mouth of Poulmorland to Bodenek village half a mile, wher the passage is to Fawy ...'[26]

Poul-morlande, Poulmorland or Polmorland, also seen in the forms Polmorla, Polmorle, Polmort and Polmorte, was clearly the Cornish name for Mixtow, the derivation of which is itself Anglo-Saxon.[27] Places on the coast, visited by English sailors, often had names in both languages. A good example is Mevagissey, the Cornish name for what English sailors called Portillie. Several of the main ports of Cornwall, including Padstow and Wadebridge, have usually been known in modern times by what are English names.* Fowey itself seems to have taken its name from *fagus*, the Latin for beech tree, rather than anything Cornish.[28] The names of the main farms in the parish of Lanteglos, especially those near Mixtow, also have a mixture of Cornish and English names. While Essa, Lamellyon, Lanlawren, Trethake and Triggabrowne are Cornish; Castle, Churchtown, Dorset and Yeate are English. Intriguingly, a farm with land on either side of Mixtow Pill was known as 'Mixtow and Polmorland' or 'Mixtow and Polmort', giving both its Cornish and its English names into modern times.

The early history of landowning in the parish is complicated and uncertain, with the land divided between as many as eight different manors. Two of these, Threthac and Nantvat (probably the modern Trethake and Lantivet) are mentioned in Domesday Book.† The first known lord of the manor of Polruan was Philip Daubeny in the thirteenth century. The large manor of Fawitone (its name derived from the River Fowey), belonging to the Wylingtones in the fourteenth century, stretched well beyond Lanteglos. The other manors were Bodinnick, Lamellyon, Lanlawren and Tolcarne. Mixtow may have been in the manor of Tolcarne, also known as Carne. A document of 1390 mentions Lombard, just above Mixtow, as being in this manor.[29]

---

* The names for Padstow and Wadebridge in Cornish are Lannwedhenek and Ponswad. Falmouth's recent attempt to acquire a second identity as Aberfala is based on adding the Welsh word for river mouth to the river's name, rather than on any authentic Cornish derivation ('heyl' is the Cornish for estuary, as in the Helford River and Hayle). Falmouth's first name seems to have been 'Smythwyk' (Smith's Village'), and then Pennicomequicke (also English). O.J. Padel, *A Popular Dictionary of Cornish Place-Names* (Penzance, 1988), pp. 83, 131, 176.

† For Domesday references to the area near Mixtow, see *Domesday Book: Cornwall*, ed. John Morris (Chichester, 1979), 2.11 (St Winnow); 5.2.22 (Penpoll); 5.2.32 (Trevelyan); 5.4.4 (Lantivet); 5.5.13 (Trethake); and 5.13.1 (Manely).

The main house in the parish was called Hall. It was on the site of what is now Hall Farm, above Bodinnick. It came into the possession of Mohun family when Reginald Mohun of Dunster married Elizabeth, the daughter and heiress of Sir John Fitzwilliam of Hall, in the early fourteenth century. There are brasses in Lanteglos Church to Reginald's son John and to his grandson Thomas. The Mohuns, who were the principal local landowners, lived at Hall until the reign of Elizabeth I, when in 1579 they moved to Boconnoc.[30]

The south of the parish, with cliffs overlooking the sea and the fine headland of Pencarrow, was windswept and rocky. According, however, to an early nineteenth-century history of the parish:

> The northern side of these lands presents a happy contrast ... Here nature wears a most mild and benignant aspect, cultivated inclosures rise in universal harmony, over the beds of transparent waters which form the haven, whose bosom is seldom violently agitated, but glides in gentle murmurs to and fro, enlivening all the diversified scenery within its regulated course.[31]

Records for the farms near Mixtow go back many centuries. In a sale of the manor of Fawitone in 1592, the names of Dorsett, Lumbard, Michaelstowe (Mixtow) and Yeate are all listed. Field names also suggest the presence there of a mill and a dovecote.[32] A fine account of Tudor Cornwall was written by Richard Carew of Antony, whose *Survey of Cornwall* was published in 1602.[33] (Dorset Farm, immediately above Mixtow House, belonged in the sixteenth century to Carew, who sold it to John Rashleigh for £250.)[34] Farming in the area was a mixture of arable and pastoral, with sheep being kept mainly for their wool. Income from farming was supplemented by other activities, including fishing and weaving. Carew recognised the hard labour needed to grow crops: 'whosoever looketh into the endeavour which the Cornish husbandman is driven to use about his tillage shall find the travail painful, the time tedious, and the expenses very chargeable ... The tillable fields are in some places so hilly that the oxen can hardly take sure footing, in some so tough that the plough will scarcely cut them, and in some so shelfy that the corn hath much ado to fasten his root'.[35]

The inventory of Robert Botters of Lombard, dating from 1638 and valued at £32 13s. 10d., contained, as well as corn and livestock, equipment for fishing and weaving:

Corn in the mowhaye	£1
Corn in the ground	£2
Fourteen sheep	£3
Two little pigs	2s.
One little boat with tackle	£3
One pair of looms	£1[36]

Botters clearly took at least a minor part in the fishing industry, which formed a large part of Fowey's industry and trade, and even more so that of Polruan and Bodinnick, with pilchards as its staple.[37] He was also a weaver.

Carew gives a vivid impression of what could be seen, in Elizabethan times, from Hall Walk above Bodinnick:

> In passing along, your eyes shall be called away from guiding your feet, to descry by their farthest kenning the vast ocean sparkled with ships that continually this way trade forth and back to most quarters of the world. Nearer home, they take view of all sized cocks, barges and fisherboats, hovering on the coast. Again, contracting your sight to a narrower scope, it lighteth on the fair and commodious haven, where the tide daily presenteth his double service of flowing and ebbing, to carry and recarry whatsoever the inhabitants shall be pleased to charge him withal, and his creeks (like a young wanton lover) fold about the land with many embracing arms.[38]

As well as using dung to enrich the soil, local farmers spread seaweed and fish waste on their fields. According to an observer is 1794:

> Long before we landed at Fowey, our olefactory nerves were assailed with the effluvia of salted pilchards. The very fields were strewed with the refuse of salt and fish, which no doubts makes excellent manure and may be obtained, we were informed, at so small a price as 9d. or 1s. per bushel, each bushel consisting of eighteen gallons.[39]

To sweeten the land, sand was brought from Lantivet:

It is usual for the neighbouring farmers to get sand at the spring tides and deposit it in a creek adjoining sandways till they think it proper to remove it, the customary payment for which to the tenant of Lantivett has always been 3s. 6d. annually for every horse employed in such removal whatever may be the quantity of sand carried off.[40]

Lime was spread to improve yields, especially from the late eighteenth century.[41] To prepare this, limestone was calcified in kilns, being heated to around 1000 degrees centigrade. As the stone and coal needed for the process were far cheaper to bring in by boat, these kilns, the remains of which can be seen throughout the area, were nearly always built near to water. Good surviving examples are at Lerryn and Pont. There is a striking drawing, dating from 1814, of a now-vanished limekiln at Mixtow, on land leased out by Philip Rashleigh in 1797. These limekilns went out of use by the mid nineteenth century, being replaced by a small number of large-scale works using the railways for distribution.[42]

By far the best known of Mixtow's early inhabitants were involved in something much more adventurous than farming, fishing or weaving. In the middle ages, members of the Mixstowe or de Michelstowe family were leading shipowners and merchants in Fowey. Their name is often spelt as Mixstowe, but whether they gave their name to Mixtow Pill or took it from it is uncertain.[43] Nor is there archaeological or other evidence for their use of Mixtow Pill as a base for their activities, though the beach immediately above Mixtow must have been useful for careening ships.[44] In 1357 Richard Mixstowe hired out a cog, a single-masted, clinker-built, flat-bottomed ship, to the Black Prince, for which he was paid £20. In 1364 William Mixstowe received a licence to export two hundred packs of white and russet cloth, and another to export a hundred barrels of hake. In 1436 John Mixstowe was given a licence to renew his private chapel in his house on the riverside at Fowey. John's daughter and heiress, Amicia, married Thomas Treffry, an early member of the family which built and still owns Place, the principal house in Fowey.[45]

The shipowning, trading, building and marital concerns of the Mixstowes or Michelstowes have, however, been overshadowed by their reputation as pirates. Their activities, in fact, were not very different from those of later sea-dogs, including Sir Francis Drake. The Mixstowes mixed legitimate trading with opportunistic piracy during the Hundred Years War, when

England was repeatedly at war with France. Virtually all the complaints about incidents of piracy, or certainly those to which the king and his council paid any attention, came from others than the French. Indeed it seems to have been unstated government policy to turn a blind eye to, and indeed to encourage, all seizures from the French. The Mixstowes' offence was that they overstepped the mark, taking advantage of the government's semi-official encouragement of piracy to seize vessels belonging to neutrals, and even at times to allies, rather than those only from France.[46]

The political turmoil at the time of the deposition of Richard II, and the longer breakdown of central government during the reign of Henry VI, also created a domestic power vacuum. This abdication of central government culminated in the Wars of the Roses, when the houses of York and Lancaster were too involved in mutual hostilities to police distant parts of the realm. Those involved in 'piracy' were not, however, marginal men, outcasts from normal society, but the leading men of Fowey. The evidence for their activities comes mainly from law cases brought for restitution by foreign merchants. How far any of these plaintiffs achieved redress is unclear. No Fowey pirates seem to have been brought to justice, let alone to have been hanged, under Richard II or Henry VI.[47]

Fowey, although it established a reputation for piracy, was by no means the only port involved: others included Bristol, Dartmouth, Plymouth and Southampton. Many Fowey men were employed in the building, fitting out and provisioning of ships, the ownership of which was divided by custom amongst a number of shareholders. Local gentlemen often invested in part-ownership of vessels.

During times of war, ships from all the southern ports were used to transport troops and to attack enemy trade. In peacetime, it proved hard to give up the temptations presented by foreign cargoes. There was also an element of tit-for-tat, as Fowey ships were themselves often seized, lawfully or unlawfully, by French ships. French ships even raided Fowey itself, notably in 1457, leading to a chain being stretched across the mouth of Fowey harbour between blockhouses at Fowey and Polruan.[48]

The Mixstowes, who were prominent figures in Fowey, were active in this illegal but profitable business over several generations.[49] Even before their emergence as pirates, Mixtow itself is mentioned in a very similar context. Following an incident at St Ives in 1346, the courts ordered a commission to investigate. Three merchants from Brussels had been driven into St Ives by a storm. Despite their having paid customs duty, a number of Cornishmen had illegally seized their ship and the wine. While the customs officer had been negotiating their return, the men had 'hoisted the sail of the ship and feloniously fled' to Wales with the wine. First of the men listed as responsible was 'Richard Johan of Fowy, master of *la Michiel of Mighelestowe*', who may well have been Richard Mixstowe. Thomas Cok of Mighelestowe was also listed as involved; as were Henry Carfur, John Kyng and Richard Kyng of Polruan; John Flemmyng, Thomas Hewychs, Robert Johan, Richard Sarre and John Triduoz of Fowey; and others from elsewhere, including Bodmin.[50]

Although Richard Mixstowe was a tax collector for both Fowey and Lostwithiel, and hired out ships to the Black Prince, he also indulged in privateering or piracy. Henry and William Mixstowe were his contemporaries. In the next generation, Mark Mixstowe, the leading figure in the family business, followed Richard's example. In the wake of numerous seizures of ships and their cargoes, Mark was ordered to appear before the king and council at Westminster. His non-appearance in June 1403 led to a direct command to come to Westminster without delay: 'To leave all else and ceasing every excuse to be in person before the king and council at Westminster on the morrow of the Purification next, in order to answer what shall by the Flemings be laid against him'.[51] Mark and other members of the Mixstowe family were also undoubtedly involved in smuggling. With other Cornish merchants, Mark Mixstowe was fined £200 in 1393 for 'having shipped to parts beyond the sea certain quantities of tin without repairing to the staple of Calais, contrary to the statute in that case published'.[52]

In the next generation, John Mixstowe took the lead. The semi-authorised nature of his activities is highlighted by a case brought by two Bretons, John Caryewe, master of *Mary of le Conquet*, and John au Neste, master of *St Dulpholl of Abervyges*, in Sepember 1430. They had both been at Penzance, where they had sold their cargoes of salt and been paid for them. They had then bought cloth with the proceeds, but a number of local men had come and seized both the cloth and their ships. Later, according to the two men's petition:

John Mixstowe of Fowey and Harry Nanskaseke of Truro had caused the ship and cloth to be arrested by the admiral's deputy, John Moure, by virtue of letters of marque granted by the duke of Britanny to Harry

Nanskaseke's father nineteen years earlier; and they were keeping the ships and cloth to the great hindrance and undoing of the petitioners.[53]

Three years later, in 1433, Mixstowe is recorded as cruising off Cape St Vincent in command of a powerful ship, the *Edward*, accompanied by a smaller ship and commanding two hundred armed men. There he captured a rich Genoese carrack, landing the crew on the Portuguese shore and bringing back the goods to Fowey. Sixteen years later the *Edward* (perhaps not the same ship), accompanied by a barge called the *Mackerell*, both of which happened to be at Plymouth, took the chance to seize the *St Antonye and St Francisse*, a galley from Barcelona sheltering there from a storm. With a cargo worth £12,000, the galley was brought back to Fowey, where the goods were widely shared amongst the local inhabitants, making them complicit in the seizure and ensuring silence at the subsequent enquiry.[54]

With the re-establishment of stable government under Edward IV, their misdeeds may have finally caught up with the citizens of Fowey. According to Carew:

> Not long after, our Fowey gallants, unable to bear a low sail, in their fresh gale of fortune, began to skum the seas with their often piracies ... as also to violate their duty at land by insolent disobedience to the prince's officers, cutting off (among other pranks) a pursuivant's ears; whereat King Edward the Fourth conceived such indignation as he sent commissioners to Lostwithiel (a town nearby), who under pretence of using their service in sea affairs, trained thither the greatest number of the burgesses; and no sooner come than laid hold on, and in hold, their goods were confiscated, one Harrington executed, the chain of their haven removed to Dartmouth, and their wonted jollity transformed into a sudden misery ...[55]

It is, however, unclear how much of this actually happened, as Richard Harrington appears in several sources after the date of his supposed hanging. Piratical activities seem also to have continued largely unabated.

While Fowey has always had an active maritime history, its distance from the heart of government in London meant that it was seldom directly involved in national events. Although Tywardreath Priory, near St Blazey, was seized by Henry VIII as part of the Dissolution of the Monasteries, neither Fowey nor Lanteglos was involved in the west country Prayer Book Rebellion of 1549. War with Spain was nearly brought about in December 1568, however, by the controversial seizure of treasure, worth £400,000, being sent by Philip II to pay his troops in the Netherlands. The ships carrying it had put in to Fowey and Saltash to avoid French privateers. At Fowey thirty-two cases, each with 20,000 reals in it, were taken off two pinnaces by the Spanish crew and 'carried to the house of Mr John Treffry and there locked and sealed with their seals and ours, and four or six of the Spaniards with some of our men with watch guarding the same did remain until her grace's commandment'.[56] Although the treasure was opened and counted, and then taken under heavy escort to London, in the end it was returned to Spain.

Philip Rashleigh, the younger son of a Barnstaple merchant, settled in Fowey in 1529. The Rashleighs, who in 1545 bought the manor of Trenant on the Gribbin peninsula, previously owned by Tywardreath Priory, were the leading merchants in Fowey during the reign of Elizabeth I and also engaged profitably in privateering. John Rashleigh (1552–1624) started building a house near the Gribbin at Menabilly. This was completed by his son, Jonathan Rashleigh (1591–1675). In time the Rashleighs acquired so much land on both sides of the river that it gave them very considerable influence in deciding parliamentary elections for the borough of Fowey over the next two centuries.[57] During this period, and indeed until 1913, Mixtow was counted as part of Fowey for electoral purposes.[58] Fowey, however, lost its two parliamentary seats in the Reform Act of 1832, one of a number of Cornish pocket boroughs to disappear.*

After war with Spain finally broke out in 1585, Fowey made a contribution to the defeat of the Armada, the left wing of which sailed past its harbour on the afternoon of 19 July 1588. The *Francis of Foy*, belonging to John Rashleigh, which had earlier sailed with Martin Frobisher to the west of Greenland and with Drake to the West Indies, stood ready for action in the harbour. Although prevented by the wind from leaving Fowey until after the Armada had passed by, the *Francis* then played its part in harrying the Spanish fleet to its destruction.[59]

An exception to the usual isolation of Cornwall was during the

---

* Before the changes made by the Reform Act, Cornwall had no less than forty-four parliamentary seats. Fowey's parliamentary seats dated from 1571.

English Civil War, when Parliament suffered its most humiliating defeat nearby in 1644. A sizeable Parliamentarian army, under the Earl of Essex, was trapped by Royalist forces in Lostwithiel. Without supplies, and surrounded by the king's troops on the east bank of the river and by those of Sir Richard Grenville to the west, the Parliamentarians fell back on Fowey, which they had earlier captured, in the hope of being taken off by sea. Royalist guns sited at Polruan made this impossible. Deserted by Essex, who escaped to Plymouth in a fishing boat, the remnant under Philip Skippon surrendered at Castle Dore on 2 September 1644.[60]

Charles I himself had a lucky escape not far from Mixtow. According to one of his officers, Richard Symonds, on 17 August 1644 the king, having first visited Cliff, between Lerryn and Penpoll, went to observe Fowey, held by Parliamentarian troops, from Hall Walk:

> His Majestie attended with his owne troop, Queene's troope, commanded by Captain Brett and sixty troopers, went to Cliffe, a parish on this side of the river that runs to Listithiel, where Colonel Lloyd, the Quarter-Master Generall's regiment lyes to keepe the passe. The enemye keepes the passe on the other side at the parish of Glant. From thence his Majestie went to Lanteglos, to the manor howse belonging to Lord Mohun just over against Foye, where his royall person ventred to goe into a walke there, which is within halfe musket shott from Foye, where a poor fisherman was killed in looking over, at the same time that his Majestie was in the walke and in the place where the King a little afore passed by.[61]

Essex's troops had already sacked Menabilly, as a house belonging to Royalist owners, the Rashleighs, and had severely damaged Hall, the Mohuns' house at Bodinnick.[62]

By the end of the seventeenth century the two main landowners in Lanteglos, and in Mixtow, were the Mohuns of Hall and Boconnoc, and the Rashleighs of Menabilly. In 1712, however, Charles, fourth Lord Mohun, fought a sensational duel in Hyde Park in which both he and his opponent, the fourth Duke of Hamilton, were killed.[63] Mohun's widow, Elizabeth, sold Boconnoc and its surrounding land to Thomas 'Diamond' Pitt for £54,000. Pitt, who had made an immense fortune in India, had gained his nickname from the acquisition of the famous Pitt diamond in Madras, which he sold to the Duke of Orleans for £135,000 in 1717. The

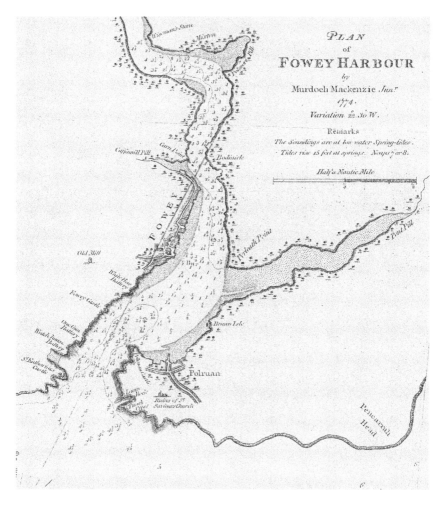

Naval Chart of Fowey Harbour, 1774, by Murdoch Mackenzie. (*Private Collection*)

diamond ended up as part of Napoleon's imperial sceptre. Pitt was the grandfather and great-grandfather of two Prime Ministers, William Pitt the Elder and his son, William Pitt the Younger.[64] The Boconnoc Estate later descended to the Grenville family and then to the Fortescues.

Although Fowey Harbour was used by a great variety of ships, it was of particular concern to the Royal Navy. As early as 1540, Henry VIII commissioned an ambitious survey of the coast of south-west England, from Exeter to Land's End, as part of a review of its defences against the

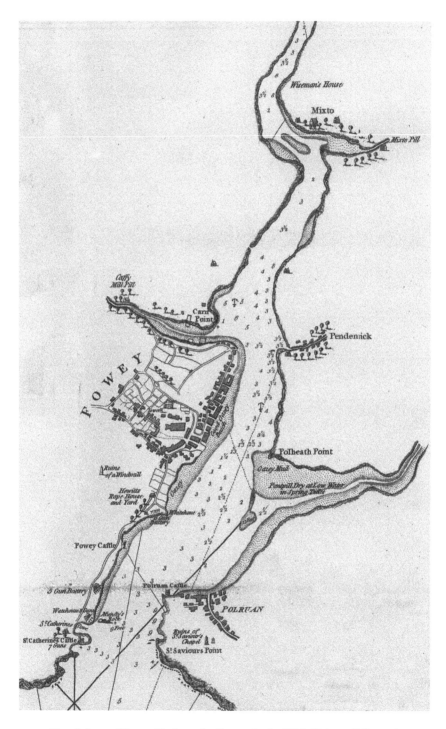

Naval chart of Fowey Harbour, by James Cook, 1786. (*Private Collection*)

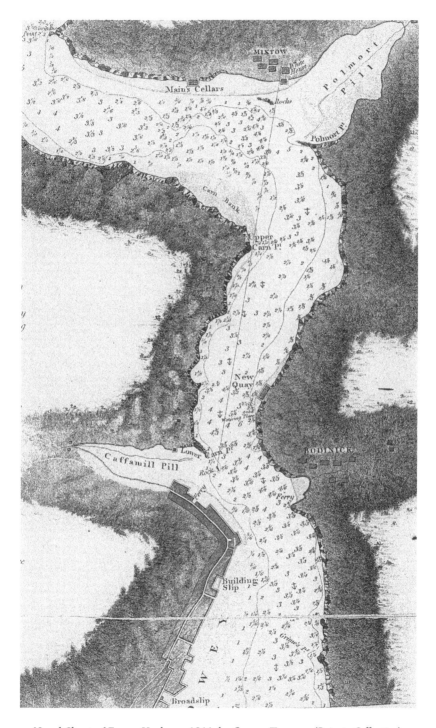

Naval Chart of Fowey Harbour, 1811, by George Thomas. (*Private Collection*)

threat of French invasion (plate 1).[65] Based on information supplied by the different ports, it presents a vivid image of Fowey and its river, but it cannot be said to be strictly accurate. Mixtow Pill, in a moment of glory, is shown as larger than the inlets of Lerryn and Penpoll, which are in reality much larger.

From the eighteenth century, Britain's naval interests were mirrored by the production of accurate charts of Britain's coastline and ports. These give accurate soundings and a reliable outline of the harbours surveyed. Drawn up by expert hydrographers, of whom Captain Cook was the greatest, they were far less interested in the buildings and other land features than in the depth of the water and the sites of rocks and of other nautical hazards.[66]

Two such charts of Fowey Harbour were plotted in the second half of the eighteenth century.[67] The first was by Lieutenant Murdoch Mackenzie junior RN in 1774. Naming Mixtow Pill as 'Polmort Pill', it misnames the area behind a clearly visible quay as 'Mixton', showing three buildings there. Another building, on the site of Watty's boathouse, lies behind a second quay. Two houses are shown at Merrifield. A second survey, by Lieutenant James Cook, RN, was printed in 1786. This was not the famous Captain Cook, who had died on Hawaii in 1779, but his eldest son. Cook names Mixtow as 'Mixto', showing two houses but no quays, and a house at Merrifield. Mackenzie shows the point above Mixtow as Wiseman's Stone, while Cook merely names the area behind it as Wiseman's House.[68]

Two detailed charts, with better views of the buildings surrounding the harbour, were issued in 1811 and 1813. The first survey, dedicated by its sponsor Reginald Pole Carew 'to the Mayor and Free Burgesses of Fowey', was made by George Thomas. It names Mixtow Pill as Polmort Pill, with Polmort Point at its southern exit. Mixtow is given its modern spelling and has five rectangles representing buildings near the quay. Two houses are also shown at Merrifield. The chart shows both quays, naming one on the later site of Watty's boathouse as 'Main's Cellars'. The second chart, 'A Survey of Fowey Harbour' was 'respectfully presented to the Merchants of the United Kingdom' by Joseph Thomas Austen, later Treffry, in 1813. It differs from the 1811 chart in naming Mixtow Pill as Polmorland Pill and in showing an old quay near what it terms Polmorland Point. Main's Cellars are shown, more correctly, as Mein's Cellars and the indent in the bank of the pill is described as a timber pond. It also shows an old wall near Polmorland Point and two houses at Merrifield.

Mein's Cellars, the later site of Watty's boathouse, were not cellars in the sense of being below ground level, impractical in such close proximity to the river. The cellars were used to salt, smoke and pack the pilchards, and a variety of other fish, which had been caught. (These cellars were also known, in a somewhat unlikely way, as 'pallices' or 'palaces'; one such giving its name to a beach near Lantivet.) The fish were laid in walls or 'bulks', then pressed into barrels, either pickled in brine or smoked. There had been earlier cellars had been in Fowey and Polruan, but pressure on space there led to the construction of cellars away from them. Mein's Cellars were only one of a number of cellars along the Fowey estuary. Two other nearby cellars were Prime Cellars, opposite Fowey, and New Quay Cellars (later Hunkin's Yard) between Bodinnick and Mixtow. Polmorte Quay may also have been the site of a fish cellar.[69] Mixtow Dock, nearby, was certainly used as a timber pond. Timber was floated in and held for seasoning inside the dock. It was then sent on to sawmills by raft.[70]

2

Houses and Farms

AS A FARMING community, cut off by the river from the nearest town and with no public buildings, it is unsurprising that Mixtow has had little in the way of public history for most of its existence. The absence of crime and of other sensations, if the distant piratical activities of the Mixstowes are allowed to fade, does not mean that Mixtow has no history.* Land tenure and house ownership, and the proximity of the river, all generated records. Of these records the most substantial are sales, leases and agreements about land rights. Other information survives in advertisements in the local papers; in census records; and in maps, both naval and terrestrial.

A valuable early source, though it only covers part of Mixtow, is a Boconnoc Estate terrier (a list of fields and their extent) drawn up, with a map, to go with the advertisement of three farms.[1] This dates from 1814,

---

* A report in the *Royal Cornwall Gazette*, 19 November 1870, gives an idea of the usual run of local news: 'A valuable cow, belonging to Mr James Rundle of Bodinnoc, fell over the cliff at Mixtow, Fowey Harbour, on Sunday last and was killed on the spot'. Earlier in the century John Couch had reported the theft of a cow: 'Mickstow, brown cow strayed or stolen, very old. Whoever brings cow or information to John Couch at Mixtow will be handsomely rewarded and all reasonable expenses paid', *Royal Cornwall Gazette*, 29 December 1804. Not all such news of losses, however, concerned cows. Two men from Mixtow, William Lamb senior in 1855 and Edward Atkinson in 1911, were drowned.

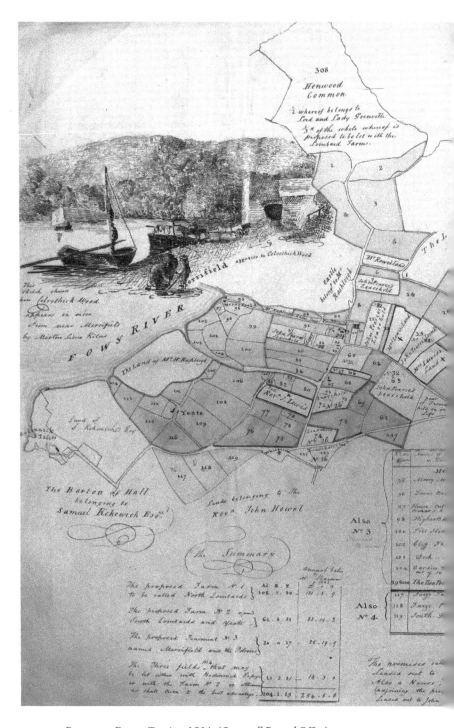

Boconnoc Estate Terrier, 1814. (*Cornwall Record Office*)

The proposed Lombard Farm
N.º 1

Proposed Yeate Farm
N.º 2

N.º on Plan	Names of House or Field	Quantity A. R. P.	N.º Share Valuation	as formerly belonging to the Tenement	N.º on Plan	Names of House or Fields	Quantity A. R. P.	N.º Share Valuation	as formerly belonging to the Tenement
1	Wall Park				63				Marks
2	Hollwell Park				69	Middle Floor			
3	Lower Park				73	Farge Park			
4	Otte Park				227	Outside			
5	New Park				124	Anglet			
6	Castle Hays			Beates	75	Ball Park			Hundred
7	Pearces Leasoh				74	Higher Brensthorn			Twinfloor
8	Lombard Atwotten				77	Lower Brensthorn			
9	Above Town Mead				78	East Park			Hundred
11	Higher Meadow				79	Grey Meadow			
13	The Slip			Marks	80	Above Town			Twinfloor
14	Above Town Croom				81	House Garden			
16	Higher Lombard			Beates	82	Orchard			
17	Lower Down				83	Little Meadow			
19	Hankyns Lower Down			Hankyns	105	the Orchard			
20	Higher Lombard Farm			Marks and Twinfloor	128	Hill Park			
21	Lower do.			do.	127	Orchard in do.			
22	Lombard Downhill			do.	108	Lea Close			
60	Great Garman			Larchischall	109	Above Town			
64	Hays Park			Marks	110	Small Yard Green			Yeate
68	Above Town			do.	111	Higher Meadow			
67	Buildings Orch.			do.	112	Lower Meadow			
84	Underton Cooke			Hankyns	113	Lushey Floor			
85	Unh. Jase Town			Marks	114	Lushey Hundred			
86	Moray Meadow			Do.	115	Middle Close			
90	House Hous & orchot			Beates	116	Three Corners Park			
91	Her Garton								
93	Fore Meadow			Towns Floor					
94	Well House			do.					

though the valuations were those made by an early valuer, Mr Sharman, in 1806. The leases were advertised in June 1814:

Very Desirable Farms and Premises in the Parish of Lanteglos Adjoining and Contiguous to the River Fowey. To be let for Seven or Fourteen Years from Michaelmas next.

	Acres	Rods	Perches
North Lombards Farm containing	108	2	30
South Lombards and Yate	61	3	2
Merrifield and the Polroses	20	0	7
The Three South Parks	13	2	31
Total	13	2	31^2

The terrier lists all the fields on three farms to be called North Lombards; South Lombards and Yate; and Merrifield and the Polroses; plus three additional fields 'that may be let either with Bodinnick Passage or with the Farm no. 2 or otherwise as shall turn to the best advantage'. In addition, other fields inside the Boconnoc Estate holding in Mixtow are shown as leased out to Mr Pearce, on a term of three lives, or as belonging to Mr Rowe and the Reverend John Howel. A field to the south of Lombard farmhouse is listed as belonging to the late Reverend John Lewis and two others to Mrs Lewis.*

Farm No. 1, to be called North Lombards, was of 108 acres and was valued at £2623 and at an annual rent of £131 3s. 9d. Farm No. 2, South Lombards, was of 61 acres and valued at £1679 and an annual rent of £83 19s. 2d; while Farm No. 3, Merrifield and the Polroses, of 23 acres, was valued at £519 and at annual rent of £25. The rent under the leases was clearly chargeable at 5 per cent per annum. Farm No. 1, North Lombards, corresponds largely with the later Lombard Farm; while Farm No. 2 corresponds to Yeate Farm, though without Polmorland or Polmorte

---

* It is easy to get muddled between the various Lombard farms. The North Lombards Farm of the 1814 advertisement was what was subsequently generally known as Lombard Farm. The South Lombards Farm of the 1814 advertisement was subsequently known as Yeate Farm. Another, smaller farm, not owned by the Boconnoc Estate but centred on the house now known as South Lombard, consisted of land owned by the Reverend John Lewis and his wife. The land belonging to this third farm was bought by Leslie Brown for his son, Dick, in the 1960s and is now part of Dorset Farm.

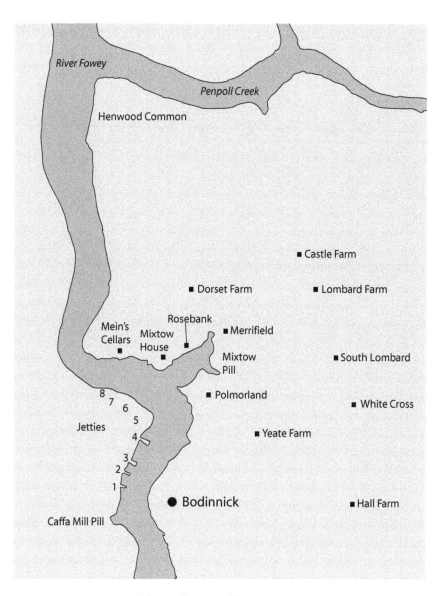

Mixtow farms and Fowey jetties

Farm. Two fields called the Polroses made up almost half of Farm No. 3, Merrifield and the Polroses, which also included a Dock Field of two acres bordering the timber pond on the south side of Mixtow Pill. Castle Farm is shown as 'belonging to Mr Rashleigh'. What is clear over time is that, while the traditional farms were very long lasting, the land they farmed under successive leases varied considerably.

Because it covers the whole parish and gives substantial detail, allowing the position of each field and house to be identified on an accompanying map, the Tithe Redemption survey begun in 1839 is the earliest full record of Mixtow. Drawn up under legislation requiring every parish to provide exact land valuations, its aim was to allow tithes in kind, payment of which was a highly contentious issue, to be converted into monetary rents. The agreement for Lanteglos by Fowey was reached on 7 August 1839, but the final version of the return was not signed off until 13 September 1845.[3] The information on it can be used both retrospectively, to shed light on earlier holdings and agreements; and prospectively, to make sense of later ones. A summary, which noted that the roads in Lanteglos by Fowey were 'very bad and very hilly', reported that there were 102 horses, 420 cows and bullocks, and 1700 sheep in the parish.[4]

The census returns from 1841 to 1911 supply a wealth of names and ages, plus the place of birth, of those living in Mixtow. There were three main farming dynasties. At Dorset, called for a time Lazzard Farm, three generations of William Lambs followed one another. A younger Charles Varcoe followed his father, also Charles Varcoe, at Lombard. The farm was then taken over by a nephew, born in Kent, John Colin Ferris. At Yeate, after John Box, Herbert Carnall was followed by his son, Richard. Castle Farm, in contrast, which was owned by the Lambs, was usually occupied by agricultural labourers, as were three cottages belonging to Lombard Farm. South Lombard, however, was independently owned and run as a small farm.

The Tithe Redemption map shows the roads and paths in and near Mixtow at the time of the survey. Many of these were undoubtedly ancient. No road ran from the ferry at Bodinnick other than up through the village street: only a path led towards Yeate Farm and Polmorland from the landing. The main road to the outside world was from the top of Bodinnick, past Hall Farm.[5] Two lanes, from White Cross and Highway, led down to Lombard and Castle Farms. The main approach to the waterside at Mixtow was the lane down from Lombard to the head of the pill, with a way for wagons then following the north bank of the pill towards Mixtow House, before turning up to Dorset Farm. There was a path, enlarged for only part of the way into a lane, between Dorset and Castle Farms.

Besides detailed information about the main farms, the Tithe Redemption register provides information about other farms and landholdings in Mixtow. John Glanville, besides Castle Farm, farmed Norbruns, fields belonging to Emma Norbrun bordering the eastern end of Penpoll, and another small farm, Henwood and Daws Lombard. There were several smaller holdings. The twelve acres near White Cross shown in 1816 as belonging to the late Reverend John Lewis, were owned in the 1840s by Matthew Bunney and described at Butter's Tenement in Lombard, including a cottage which subsequently became the present South Lombard. John Hicks leased the three acres at Butter's House, where he lived. (This was the later site of Windrush Cottage and Lombard Cottage.) Another twelve acres, Henwood and Whitacross, leased by John Climo from the Boconnoc Estate, were occupied by Nicholas Hoskins. Finally, Henwood Common, at the end of a lane running from Castle Farm to above the western end of Penpoll, and without either a house or barn on it, was split between five different farms.*

By the late middle ages, most obvious sites adjacent to water had been taken for houses.[6] The appeal of a superb position, just above the town of Fowey, makes it very likely that there was a house on the site of Mixtow House from an early date. What any earlier house looked like is unknown, but it is clear that the present Mixtow House has been updated repeatedly around an ancient core.[7] The written records also make clear that the present house, with its Georgian façade, is the oldest house on the banks of the pill itself. With its striking view down the harbour towards Polruan, the house was originally the farmhouse of Mixtow Farm, with an adjacent cluster of farm buildings. The tenants of Mixtow Farm also nearly always held the land and farm buildings on the opposite side of the pill. Although legally separate, the two farms are often referred to by the joint name of Mixtow and Polmorland. Mixtow House, which is

---

* Henwood Common, shown as half owned by the Boconnoc Estate in the terrier of 1814, had fields on it farmed by John Glanville of Henwood and Daws Lombard, Nicholas Hoskins of Henwood and Whitacross, William Lamb of Dorset and Charles Varcoe of North Lombard. Part of Glanville's holding was of nine acres belonging to Thomas Robins. There was also a turning off to the right after Castle Farm on the lane to Henwood Common. This led to a mowhay (a barn) on Norbruns.

accessible, unlike most of the pill, at all but the lowest tides was often leased out, as a separate villa, from the early nineteenth century, leaving Mixtow Farm only its farm cottage.

As has been seen, the earliest mention of Mixtow in legal documents dates back to 1409. There must have been many similar documents over the following hundred and eighty years, but none survives. The next surviving legal document is from the end of the sixteenth century. 'Michellstow' is mentioned in a transaction of 1592 by which Reynolde Mohun bought part of the manor of Lanteglos by Fowey from Thomas Beaumont of Straughton, Leicestershire, and his brother, Huntington Beaumont of the Inner Temple. In 1607 John Hunkins senior and John Hunkins junior sold lands in 'Mixto alias Mihelstowe', previously leased by William Marke, Raphe and Margery Marke, John Michell and Thomas Hellyar, to John Rashleigh of Fowey. Later in the seventeenth century Jonathan Rashleigh leased Mixtow to Thomas Hellyar in 1629, to Richard Hellyar in 1634, to Boaten Bottors in 1645 and Edward Chappell in 1692.*

The last of these agreements, a ninety-nine lease granted by Jonathan Rashleign to Edward Chappell on 6 June 1692, by which Chappell under-took to pay a premium of £25 and a rent of £2 a year, mentions 'that messuage, tenement or dwelling house which one John Michell built, together with one orchard adjoining the same, one meadow and one little quillett of land, which lyeth in the lane above the house of John Botteres and pasture for one pigg'. John Michell held Mixtow during the reign of Elizabeth I, before John Hunkins, whose lease, dating from Lady Day in 1592, describes Mixtow as being occupied by Michell.[8]

In a ninety-nine year lease dated 22 February 1719, between Jonathan Rashleigh, John Goodall and Gregory Stribley at a payment of 10s. per year, a house is mentioned in similar terms as

the messuage and tenement situate lying and being at Mixtow within the parish of Lanteglos in the County of Cornwall now or late in the possession of Richard Bottors. And hereinafter particularly mentioned (that is to say) all the dwelling houses and outhouses thereto belonging to the small orchard plot and Bottors. And hereinafter particularly mentioned (that is to say) all the dwelling houses and outhouses

---

* Cornwall Record Office, R/1964–68. See also R/1677. The spelling of surnames and place-names varies in different deeds: for instance, Botters, Bottors, Botteres or Butters; Mitchell or Michell; Polmorle, Polmorte, Polmorla or Polmorland.

thereto belonging to the small orchard plot and a certain courtilage or linney adjoining to the strand and also a small quillett of ground thereto adjoining with their and every of their appurtenances.[*]

On 19 November 1725 Gregory Stribley, described as a merchant of Fowey, assigned a lease at Mixtow to a cooper, John Row, on the receipt of £50. It granted 'lands, tenements, meadows, fields, closes and parcels of land and the apputenances situate lying and being in at Mixtow alias Mighistow ... in the several occupation of William Hunkin, John Bon and Peter Trubody' and 'the messuage or dwelling house lying and being at Mixtow aforesaid now in the possession or occupation of one Margarett Botters'.[9]

By the late eighteenth century, when Richard Bennett held the lease of Mixtow from the Rashleigh estate, details about Mixtow House appear in the advertisement of a lease for fourteen or twenty-one years from Michaelmas 1795:

> All that messuage or dwelling house called Mixtow House, pleasantly situated on the banks of the River Fowey, with the gardens and appur-tenances thereto belonging. And also all those lands and tenements adjoining, and occupied therewith by Mr Richard Bennett, called Mixtow and Polmorland, situate in Lanteglos by Fowey. A survey will be held at the house of Walter Colmer, innkeeper, in Fowey, Saturday the third day of May.

As a result, the house and land associated with it was let to John Couch, of Talland, for the term of twenty-one years.[10] The agreement was signed on 20 August 1795:

> This indenture, made the twentieth day of August in the year of our Lord one thousand seven hundred and ninety-five between Philip Rashleigh of Menabilly in the county of Cornwall Esquire, of the

---

[*] Cornwall Record Office, R/1969. The sites of the 'dwelling houses' mentioned in in this lease cannot be ascertained with any degree of certainty. Two of the oldest house sites at Mixtow are Mixtow House itself and Butter's Tenement, where a later farm cottage has massive foundations, suggesting a larger early building. Information on Butter's Tenement, later Bunt's Cottage and now Windrush Cottage, from Dave Baker.

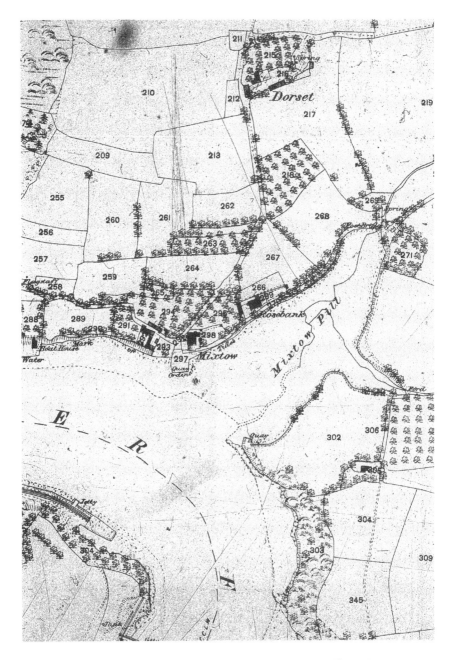

Ordnance Survey map of Mixtow, 1867. (*Private Collection*)

one part, and John Couch of the parish of Talland in the said county gardiner, of the other part, witnesseth that the said Philip Rashleigh, in consideration of the yearly rent, covenants, considerations, exceptions and agreements herewith contained and on the part of the said John Couch his executors, administrators and assigns to be yielded, paid, done, observed and performed, hath granted demised and leased and by these presents doth grant, demise and release unto the said John Couch his executors, administrators and assigns all that dwelling house called Mixtow House, with the buildings, gardens, fields, orchards and appurtenances thereunto belonging situate, lying and being at Mixtow in the parish of Lanteglos by Fowey in the said county heretofore purchased by the said Philip Rashleigh of and from John Mitchell Gentleman. And also all that messuage and tenement commonly called and known by the name of Polmorland situate, lying and being in the parish of Lanteglos by Fowey aforesaid.[11]

In 1797 Philip Rashleigh issued a ninety-nine year lease to three men to build a limekiln at Mixtow, including the use of the quay, at an annual rent of half a guinea.[12] The three tenants were John Couch, of Mixtow House and Farm, and two yeomen of Lanteglos by Fowey, John Cossentine and Robert Ream. The men worked the kiln until 1820, when they sold the lease to Richard Salt, a mariner from Polruan, for £25.[13]

John Couch's lease to Mixtow and Polmorland expired in 1816, when two agents for William Rashleigh, Edward Roberts and John Parker, estimated the dilapidations on the farms at £59 14s. 5d. The house, at that point tenanted by Captain Nicholas Eveleigh, was again advertised on 6 October 1832:

To be let by tender, for a term of seven to fourteen years, at the option of either landlord or tenant from Michaelmas next, the cottage or dwelling house of Mixtow, consisting of two ground rooms, kitchen, pantry, dairy and cellar, and five bedrooms and a closet with suitable outhouses and about twelve acres of good orchard, pasture, and tillable land. Also to be let therewith or separately Polmorland adjoining, consisting of a good barn, stable and cow house and about seventeen acres of good orchard, pasture, and arable land.

Mixtow is a most desirable residence for a bachelor, or a small genteel family, being situated immediately on the beautiful river and harbour of Fowey, and within a quarter of a mile of the town of Fowey, and lies in the parish of Lanteglos. For viewing the premises apply to Captain Eveleigh, the present tenant.

The Tithe Redemption register provides detailed information about the land making up the two holdings at Mixtow and Polmorland Farm. Mixtow, totalling 17 acres 2 roods and 23 perches, included the house, garden and orchard; a yard and 'sites'; and the road, a quay and 'waste'. The fields were Lower Mixtow Hill (marked as arable land), Upper Mixtow Hill, Cliff Terrace Meadow, Wiseman's Stone, West Park, Slad Park and another orchard. These fields bordered the river from the end of Mixtow Pill to just above Wiseman's Stone, though they were interrupted by five small pieces of land belonging to other holders.[14] Four other fields, Bramble Hill, Three Plots, Middle Field and Begores, lay slightly back from the river.

Polmorland, on the southern bank of Mixtow Pill, came to 10 acres, 1 rood and 32 perches, all in one block. Its fields were Higher Ground, Middle Ground, Pill Ground, Home Way Field, Outer Way Field and Lower Ground. It included a wood bordering the river to the south of Polmorland or Polmorte Point, 'farm houses', two yards and the lane running up from the end of the creek. The 'farm houses' were farm buildings, not dwelling houses, as there is no evidence of anybody having lived at Polmorland.

Although both shared occupiers and owners over the years, the history of Polmorland differs from that of Mixtow and the title to it remained distinct. It was leased by John Treffry to John Michell in 1573. In 1616 Reynold Michell bought or renewed the lease for £40. Treffry leased Polmorland to John Marke in 1648 and then to Simon Trubody in 1671. In 1684, however, John Treffry sold the manor of Polvethan, including Polmorland, as well as other property in Lanteglos, Lansallos and St Veep, to Jonathan Rashleigh for £1600. Philip Rashleigh then leased Polmorland to Gregory Stribley in 1728.[15] In 1795 John Couch took on the lease of Mixtow and Polmorland, though the latter still seems to have been occupied by Richard Bennett in 1805.

The Tithe Redemption register shows both Mixtow and Polmorland as owned by William Rashleigh but as occupied by William Lamb, who also farmed Dorset and Castle Farms. Lamb is recorded as the occupier of all of these in the Land Tax assessment returns for thirty years from the 1830s.* He seems to have lived at Dorset Farm and to have rented out Mixtow House. Soon after acquiring the lease of Mixtow and Polmorland, Lamb sold off mature timber on all three farms: 148 elms, thirty sycamores and one ash 'To be sold by public auction, at the house of Edward Roberts, in St Veep Church-Town, on Wednesday the second day of January next, precisely at two o'clock in the afternoon'.[16] Of these trees, fifty one were on Mixtow Farm and forty-seven on Polmorland. 'The elm timber is well adapted for ship and boat building, and all the trees are standing in lands adjoining the harbour of Fowey. For viewing apply to Mr William Lamb, the tenant, at Dorset, and further particulars to Mr Robins, solicitor, Liskeard, or to William Searle, auctioneer, Lanreath'.[17] As ship-building in Fowey, Polruan and Bodinnick was at its height during the first half of the nineteenth century, suitable timber for ships was at a premium.[18]

William Lamb's wife, Ann, died at Mixtow in 1844.[19] His father, Benjamin Lamb, died two years later, when William and his brother Joseph were executors:

> All persons indebted to the estate of Mr Benjamin Lamb, late of Fowey, deceased, are desired forthwith to pay the same to his executors, Mr Joseph Lamb, of Polgreen, in the parish of St Veep, or Mr William Lamb, of Mixtow, in the parish of Lanteglos by Fowey, and persons having any claim on the estate are requested to send the particulars thereof to one of the above-named executors, in order that the same may be adjusted and settled.[20]

In 1855, William Lamb himself died. On the evening of 9 September, 'Mr W. Lamb, of Mixtow, an old and respectable inhabitant of the parish of Lanteglos by Fowey, had some reason for hauling his boat near to the quay, when by some unfortunate cause, he fell into the water and was drowned'.† He was succeeded on the farm by his son, another William.‡

---

* According to the 1841 census, William Lamb, then aged sixty, was living at Dorset with his wife Ann and five children.

† *Royal Cornwall Gazette*, 14 September 1855. Perhaps he had a heart attack.

‡ According to the 1861 census, the younger William was living at Dorset with his wife, Elizabeth, and three children, the youngest of whom was also called William.

In 1861, Mixtow House was again advertised to let, together with Mixtow and Polmorland:

> Desirable residence near the sea, with small farm, to be let. To be let
> by tender, for a term of fourteen years, from Michaelmas next, all
> that dwelling house and those two desirable tenements, now held
> as one farm, called Mixtow and Polmorland. Situate in the parish
> of Lanteglos by Fowey; with necessary and commodious outbuild-
> ings, and comprising about 37 acres 0 roods and 15 perches of arable,
> meadow and pasture land, and orchards, now in the occupation of
> Hugh Henwood, Esquire. The house is situate on and commanding a
> view of the harbour of Fowey, and possesses superior accommodation;
> a considerable sum having been expended in improvements within the
> last few months; and the premises are in thorough order and condition.
> The above offers a most favourable opportunity to persons desiring a
> genteel residence near the sea, in conjunction with a small farm.
>
> The taker will be required to pay all rates, taxes, tithe rent charge,
> and other outgoings (except landlord's property tax) payable in
> respect of the premises, and to keep and leave the same premises in
> good repair, and to enter into a lease containing the covenants usually
> inserted in leases granted by William Rashleigh Esquire, such lease to
> be prepared by the lessor's solicitors at the taker's expense.
>
> The tenant will shew the premises, and further particulars may be
> known on application to Mr W.E. Geach, Penhellick, Tywardreath, or to
> Messrs Coode, Shilson and Co., solicitors, St Austell, by whom tenders
> will be received until the 18th day of July next, soon after which the
> person whose tender is accepted will have notice thereof.[21]

Hugh Henwood was a colourful character. With connections in the neighbouring parish of St Veep, he had made a fortune in the West Indies, where he had been a member of the Executive and Legislative Council of Grenada. After living at Mixtow between 1858 and 1861, and recovering from a bout of mental illness, he married and moved to Somerset. Henwood's death, in 1866, led to a dispute over his will:

> Dr Swabey, for the plaintiff, said he had been a native of Cornwall,
> and in early life went out to Grenada in the service of Thomason,
> Hawkes and Company, and returned to England in 1858. He lived in

Cornwall till the year 1861. He went out again but before that he was placed under restraint in the Bodmin Asylum. On coming out he went again to the West Indies, but soon returned, and then went to settle in Somersetshire near an old friend named James Langdon. He had married Miss Clark, and went to live at Ellicombe House. He died on 17 October 1866, by his own hand, so that there was of course the necessity for an enquiry into his state of mind. He made a will on the 2 June 1864, leaving his property to Edward Henwood, solicitor, of 33 Cross Street, Manchester, his natural son, and John Henwood, of Penpol, in St Veep, near Fowey. The plaintiffs were the next of kin under the will, the defendant being John Vanderluys Scantlebury, a nephew of the testator. He should call the attesting witnesses to the will: and also, if necessary, Mr Charles Roberts, the surgeon, if anything should arise, on cross-examination, and that gentleman would prove the state of the testator at the time he made the will.

After hearing two or three witnesses, probate was granted. The amount of the property of the testator passing under the will is about £60,000.[*]

The 1871 census shows Mixtow as being occupied by Harold Henwood, aged sixty-three, a retired farmer and widower. His daughter Mary, aged twenty-three, and son, John, aged eighteen, were living with him, with only one servant, Elizabeth Collings.

After the Henwoods, Mixtow House was occupied by the Clunes family. Thomas Clunes junior was involved with the Cornwall Minerals Railway. The transfer of Mixtow and Polmorland, to Thomas Clunes from C.E. Crighton, who presumably leased the farmland while the Henwoods lived at Mixtow House, prompted the drawing up of an inventory of what was on the farm:

A valuation of farm stock implements of husbandry and other effects on Mixtow and Polmorla in the Parish of Lanteglos by Fowey the property of C.E. Crighton Esq., valued on the 19th day of March 1878 by John Hoyle Leach and Richard Rundle of Lostwithiel and taken at the said valuation by Thomas Clunes Esq.

---

[*] *Royal Cornwall Gazette*, 7 November 1867. See also *Morning Post*, 7 November 1867: 'The will was opposed by the only son of a deceased sister who was not mentioned in the instrument; but the defendant did not appear to support his plea'.

1 mare Damsel, 2 fat bullocks, 2 dairy cows, 2 yearlings, 2 pigs, 14 ewes and 22 lambs, 1 ram sheep, 1 hog ditto, 34 fowls and some chickens, 157 pounds of wool, 4 bushels of barley, 4 bushels oats, hay and straw, ploughing, seed and tilling 3 acres of oats, mangels, turnips and potatoes, 2½ acres of grass seeds.

Cellar: about 18 hogsheads cider, 13 empty pipes, 8 empty hogsheads, 6 30-gallon casks, 4 knive horses, 2 cans, 1 tunner, gauge and taps, apple mill, vat, ropes and knives.

Implements: 1 iron harrow ploughing 1 acre of land, 12 wood hurdles, 3 stiddles, rings and chains, 2 racks, 2 moorstone rollers, chisels, wood harrow, ploughing 1½ acre, iron plough. Slide and chain, dray, tank, wheelbarrow, 2 rakes, scythe, wheeljack, cart and wheels, wagon, 2 iron pigs' troughs, 2 stone troughs, 1 wood ditto, grind stone, furnail and fittings, 3 pans, seedlip, hay knife, horse brushes and combs, pike prong, 6 rat gins. 4 corn bags, sheep shears, broom, winnowing sheet, tub and striker, Salter's patent weighing balance, ground maize, 4 chains and rings, pig killing stool, reeds, bacon rack, 4 slideless chains, 2 ladders, dung in the pit.

Dairy: 6 milk pans, 2 buckets, chainer, 2 calves' feeders, tub and pointer, scale and weights. Earthenware pan, cream basin, basket, thermometer, churn.

In dwelling house: table and form and corner cupboards, pigeon house.

At and for the sum of £330.

Witness our hands the day and date before written. Robert Rundle, John H. Leach.[22]

Thomas Clunes's father, Thomas Clunes senior, a talented engineer and entrepreneur, died at Mixtow House on 28 September 1879:

We have to record the death of Mr Thomas Clunes, formerly of Worcester, which took place at his residence near Fowey, on Sunday 28 ult. Mr Clunes was a native of Aberdeen and was born in the year 1815. While still a young man he came to England and settled in Worcester, where he acquired, about twenty-five years ago, an engineering concern, which was developed into the Vulcan Ironworks, of which Mr Holland (present Mayor of Worcester) is a proprietor. Mr Clunes' inventive ability and engineering knowledge were considerable. At the Great Exhibition of 1851 some mechanical appliances, originated and shown by him, were judged of such value that three medals were awarded to them. Under his direction the Vulcan works grew and prospered, and have become one of the largest concerns in the city. Mr Clunes achieved an honourable independence, and retired some years ago from the firm. Apart from business affairs he was little known in public life, and the knowledge of his real worth as a kind-hearted, genial and generous man was confined to a comparatively small circle of his own friends and representatives. He was a brother of Mr A. Clunes Sherriff, for many years MP for Worcester.[23] For a long while Mr Clunes' health had been failing; he was subject to severe attacks of bronchitis and heart disease, for which he has been during the last two years under the constant care of Dr Davis and Son of Fowey. Mr Clunes had been a widower nine years, and he leaves five daughters and four sons. The funeral took place on Thursday at the new cemetery of Worcester, and was largely attended. Several establishments in the city were partially closed in respect to the memory of the departed.[24]

Although the daughter of Thomas Clunes junior, Martha Tattersall Clunes, of Mixtow House, Fowey, Cornwall, was married by special licence to Arthur Francis Bare-Castlenan on 12 March 1879, the Clunes family seems to have left Mixtow not long afterwards.[25]

For at least twenty years, as recorded in the 1881, 1891 and 1901 censuses, Mixtow House was occupied by the Sloggett family. Joseph Sloggett was employed as a yachtsman by Edward Atkinson, a yachting enthusiast who lived at a nearby house, Rosebank. In 1881 Sloggett, a master mariner born in Fowey, was aged thirty-two. His wife, Mary, born in St Mabyn, was two years younger, while their son, also Joseph, was only four months old. Ten years later, three sons are listed, with Edward and John being born one year and two years after their brother Joseph. In 1885 Joseph Sloggett senior competed at the Lerryn Regatta: 'For canoes, first prize, gold pencil case value £2 2s.; second prize, silver medal, value £1 1s. Twice round the course. This race was fairly well contested. Watty of Fowey was a good first and Sloggett, of Mixtow, second'.[26] In 1898, however, Joseph Sloggett died. The notice of his death in the local paper read: 'At Mixtow, 10 September, Captain J.W. Sloggett, aged forty-nine – for nineteen years in the employment of Edward Atkinson, Rosebank, Fowey'. This gives an indication that both Atkinson and Sloggett arrived in Mixtow in about 1879.[27] In the 1901 census Joseph Sloggett junior, now twenty, is described as a steam-engine

maker and fitter, while the youngest brother John, aged seventeen, was a
carpenter's apprentice. On the night of the 1911 census, Mary Sloggett was
living there alone on 'private means'.

In 1909 Edward Atkinson bought the freehold of Mixtow and
Polmorland, including Mixtow House, from the Rashleigh estate for
£2850. He died, however, only two years afterwards, when his overall
estate was sold. Amongst the buildings at Mixtow Farm there was also
a cottage. This was usually occupied by those working on the farm. In
1861 Thomas Lavery, a farm labourer, lived there.[*] In 1881 it was occupied
by William Keeble, described as a farm bailiff.[†] In 1891 the cottage had
another farm labourer, William Wall, in it.[‡] Following the death of Joseph
Sloggett, Edward Atkinson employed another yachtsman, John Tamblin,
but he and his family lived in Mixtow Cottage rather than Mixtow Villa.[§]

In 1911 Mixtow Farm was occupied by Henry Liddon, from Shaldon
in Devon, and his wife, Laura, both aged thirty-seven. He is described
as a gardener and seems to have specialised in marketing gardening.
Between the wars, Mixtow Farm was farmed by Archie Tippett, born
in Lanteglos in 1889, and his wife, Carrie, who came from Polperro. As
well as producing vegetables and fruit in a market garden, to be sold to
visiting ships and in Fowey, the Tippetts took in paying guests.[¶] Their son,

---

[*]   The 1861 census return lists Thomas Lavery, forty-seven, born in Duloe, and
his wife, Jane, forty-four, born in St Neot. Their children were Isaac, fifteen, born
in Feock; Mary, aged twelve, and John, aged, ten, both born in Penryn; and Joseph,
aged six, born in St Veep.

[†]   The 1881 census return lists William Keeble, aged twenty-nine, born in
Pelynt, and his wife Jane, born in Lezant. Their children were Richard, five, and
William, two, both born in Pelynt. Mary Elizabeth, aged ten months, had been born
in Lanteglos. To help them, they had a general servant, Jane Liaves, aged fourteen,
born in Liskeard.

[‡]   The 1891 census lists William Wall, aged thirty-four, born in Lanteglos, and
his wife Mary, aged twenty-seven, born in Polperro. Their children were Emily, nearly
two, and William, ten months, both born in Lanteglos.

[§]   The 1901 census gives John Tamblin, yachtsman, aged thirty-five, born in
Fowey, and his wife, Rosie, aged thirty-three, born in Polruan, Their children Nora,
aged eleven, and Katie, aged nine, had been born in Fowey. John Leonard, aged three,
had been born in Polruan, and Russell, aged one, had been born in Mixtow itself. By
1911 the Tamblins had had four more children, Burnard, Howard, John and Clive.
John Tamblin senior is described as a 'gentleman's boatman'.

[¶]   Information about her grandparents, Archie and Carrie Tippett, from Betty
Davies. At the time of the 1911 census, Archie Tippett was working at Frogmore Farm

Leslie John, known as Jack, was in the Royal Navy for thirty years. Archie later built a bungalow at Lansallos, where he lived until his death in 1956. During the Second World War, Mixtow was farmed by Ernest Motton and his wife, Olive, until 1944. Ernest Motton had been born in Lerryn in 1904. Before taking on Mixtow Farm, he had worked as a gardener at Rosebank (renamed Kits House between the wars), the nearest house to Mixtow House, for its then owner, Winifred Hart.

There was another land holding at Mixtow. Like Polmorland, it was legally separate from Mixtow but usually held by whoever was occupying Mixtow House. This was known as Tonkin's. At the beginning of the eighteenth century, a quay was built at Mixtow by a Plymouth silversmith called Peter Tonkin.[28] The Tonkins were prominent Plymouth citizens and a later Peter Tonkin was mayor of Plymouth in 1798.[29] Silversmiths were often involved in the financing of other trades. While the quay was certainly used for legitimate purposes, it is unlikely that it was not used at times for landing contraband goods, as in eighteenth-century Cornwall smuggling was extremely widespread.

In 1719 Peter Tonkin leased the quay to a Fowey merchant, Gregory Stribley, for ninety-nine years, in return for a premium of £50 and for an annual payment of £1 14s. 0d. He conveyed

> all the several messuages, leases, tenements, meadows, closes and parcels of land with the appurtenances situated, lying and being at Mixtow alias Michelstow within; and which were late in the several occupations or portions of William Hunkin, John Bone, Peter Truebody, John Rowe and the Widow Willcock and all other the messuages, lands and tenements of him the aforesaid Peter Tonkin situated, lying or being at Mixtow alias Michelstow.[30]

It is unclear what exactly had belonged to Bone, Hunkin, Rowe, Trubody and the Widow Willcock, but these pieces of land were almost certainly ones that made up the other pieces owned by Tonkin. These are listed in the Tithe Redemption register as being owned by Tonkin's Representatives. In all, the holding amounted to 4 acres 1 rood and 17

as a 'horseman'. After the Tippetts and before the Mottons, Mixtow was farmed by Mr Honey.

perches: a field on Mixtow Hill; a garden with another plot beneath it; Pool Park; and Tonkin's meadow, orchard and quay.

Tonkin, or rather his representatives, continued to hold the freehold, but Stribley's lease seems to have passed to the occupier of Mixtow House and Farm, John Couch. In 1820 Couch, with two associates, John Cossentine, Robert Ream, who had worked the limekiln on the site, sold the lease to Richard Salt of Polruan for £25. The following year, however, this was surrendered by Salt, with the property then being occupied by Nicholas Eveleigh of Mixtow House.[31]

Some sort of dispute about past payments is reflected in a surviving letter from Philip Rashleigh, writing from Menabilly to a latter-day Peter Tonkin in December 1818:

> I can assure you that I have never in any way interfered with your land at Mixtow, having never received from Mr Couch one farthing of rent beyond what was stipulated to be paid for the late Mr Philip Rashleigh's freehold.
>
> Whatever demand therefore you claim under the covenants in your lease of your own tenant either for arrears of rent due, when the last life died, or for repairs, I conceive that the executor of the late Mr Philip Rashleigh must alone be answerable. If Mr Couch continued to occupy your premises after it fell into your hands by the dropping of the last life, he alone was of course accountable to you for the rent and ought to have tendered it accordingly. At all events, I have never individually or through my agents in any manner whatever interfered with the part of Mixtow which appropriated to yourself.[32]

In the Tithe Redemption register, Tonkin's quay and land are shown as being occupied by John Box, a substantial local farmer.[33]

Another landholding, Merrifield, belonging to the Boconnoc Estate, was at the end of Mixtow Pill. The history of the houses at Merrifield, unlike that of the neighbouring ones, is clearer for the eighteenth century than for the nineteenth. It seems likely that the houses at Merrifield fell into disrepair and were no longer inhabited after the middle of the nineteenth century, as there are no census returns for them after 1841. In contrast to most of the other holdings in Mixtow, the fields which formed Merrifield were compact and in a single group, to both sides of the stream leading back from the end of the pill. Its constituent fields are recognisably the same in the 1814 Boconnoc terrier, in the Tithe Redemption register of 1839–45 and in the land valuation of 1910. The fields were Lower Barn Park, Higher Barn Park, Pill Head Park, Cliff Park, Dock Close, all of which were arable. In addition there were houses, a yard and an orchard.

In 1727 Merrifield was leased to Thomas Nichols on three lives, including Thomas himself and his wife, Mary.[34] Under a 1739 will, however, the yeoman John Knight left his cousin, John Willcock, 'all my right and interest in a messuage after called Merryfield in Lanteglos by Fowey', complicated by a stipulation that Willcock should pay a £10 rent for it to his brother, William Willcock, when the latter became twenty-one. William Willcock was to 'have the house that now is upon the said estate with a garden plot and 10s. a year be paid him out of the estate for life'. He also left ten shillings to Thomas Nichols and ten shillings to his sister, Mary.[35]

In 1814 a house called Merrifield was auctioned separately from the land. At an auction to be held on 17 May at the Ship Inn, Fowey, Merrifield was offered with what remained of a ninety-nine year lease, depending on the longevity of the current occupier, Thomas Wallis, aged fifty.[36]

To let for seven or fourteen years compact desirable tenement called Merryfield against which the tide flows at high water, adjacent to North Lombard and with Henwood Common and South Lombard and Yeate. Occupied by Thomas Wallis, well situated to obtain manure and ship corn etc. by river, near Fowey Market Town. Limekiln close to Merriefield. Public survey at inn, Passage House, Bodinnick, 3 July.[37]

Samuel Wallis, aged fifty and a farmer, was living at Merrifield at the time of the 1841 census. As well as his wife, Mary, aged forty, five children aged from ten to one were there as well.

Rosebank, the second house of substance to be built on the side of the pill at Mixtow, dates from the 1830s. It first appears on the poll register of 1837 under the ownership of John Mein. Two years later, the Tithe Redemption register shows it as being owned by Mein but occupied by Robert McGuffoy, a Customs officer.* At the same time as the main villa of

---

* McGuffoy (also Guffey or Guffoy) was there at the time of the 1841 census, which lists Robert Guffey, aged fifty-two, his wife Margaret, forty-one, and three

Rosebank (or Rose Bank), a smaller cottage was built nearby, named Rose
Hill. Captain John Mein RN is shown as owning both on the return for
1843, where Rose Bank was assessed at 6s. 8d. and Rose Hill at 2s. Besides
the two houses, the property included a stable, gardens, a plantation, two
orchards, a slip and a field called Hunkyn's Park. These were not, however,
immediately next to the houses. The stable, gardens and plantation were
on the other side of Mixtow House and beyond the Mixtow Farm buildings, on the site of what later became Watty's boathouse. On one of the
early maps, the quay in front of it is shown as Mein's Cellars.[38] The plantation was a separate area of land beyond this, towards Wiseman's Point.
and one of the orchards was on the side of the road away from Rosebank
leading up to Dorset Farm. Hunkyn's Park and the other orchard were
to the north of the lane running from Mixtow Farm towards Wiseman's
Point, while two other small fields were a little further north.

The Mein family is well documented in Fowey. John Mein was the son
of Dr Thomas Mein (1750–1815), a naval physician who later inherited a
country estate, Eildon Hall in Roxburghshire. Dr Mein was appointed
inspector of hospital ships at Devonport in 1795, having joined the Navy
in 1771. His wife, Margaret, was Cornish and enjoyed living in Fowey,
where Mein became a close friend and political ally of the landowner
and industrialist Joseph Treffry of Place. Thomas Mein's daughter Susan
(1783–1866) wrote her memoirs, describing her early life in Fowey.[39] These
memoirs provide a great deal of information about the Mein family,
including about her uncle, Captain James Mein RN, who on 22 January
1809 was lost in the wreck of the *Primrose* on the Manacles, off Helston.[*]

The memoirs tell us more about John Mein's childhood than about
his later career. One of a family of two boys and eight girls, John, born
in 1789, was a boisterous character compared to his elder brother, Tom.
According to his sister, 'two boys more opposite in character there could
not be, the first so gentle and quiet, the other with almost uncontrollable
spirits, and constantly in mischief by playing tricks, but both equally

---

servants: Edward Cousins, nineteen, Mary Riddick, twenty-four, and Elizabeth
Williams, seventeen.

[*] Supposed to be one of the handsomest men in the Navy, James Mein was
known, due to his great height, as the 'Giant Midshipman', when he first joined ship,
ibid., pp. xii, 194 (portrait on facing page), 263. The loss of the *Primrose* was a double
blow to Fowey, as the *Primrose*, a brig-sloop built in 1807, was the only warship ever
to have been wholly built at Fowey.

affectionate'.[40] John survived falls from his cradle and into a dripping pan in early childhood.[41] At school at Kelso, his riding technique was unusual:

> As to John, he scarcely ever rode without tumbling off, for he was always playing tricks. Sometimes he would sit with his head towards the back of the pony, particularly in going through a village that he might make the children laugh. Betsey had very small ears, on which he would stick his hat, holding the bridle up and pretending he was playing the fiddle. He rather got into a scrape once on going to Kelso. Luckily, the coachman was with him. It happened this way. Going through a village, sitting as I have described him, with his back to her head, Betsey made a sudden dash in at the back door of a baker's shop, seized a roll off the counter and tumbled others with John on the floor, and was running off, when the coachman arrived in time to catch the pony and rescue John from the angry baker, who was pacified by being well paid for the stolen roll.[42]

None of this stopped John Mein having a successful career in the Navy, also as a surgeon. After retiring from active service, Mein became a highly respected citizen of Fowey, being elected a churchwarden of St Fimbarrus in 1843. He also shared ownership with John Hicks of Polruan of the *Royal Adelaide*, a 410-ton barque active in the transatlantic trade.[43]

In 1849 Mein advertised Rosebank:

> To be let, Rosebank cottage in Lanteglos by Fowey, beautifully situ-ated on banks of the river leading to Lostwithiel with pleasing view of harbour of Fowey and within twenty minutes walk of the town. Cottage etc., well adapted for a gentleman's residence; it is replete in every convenience. Delightful scenery and hills and valleys around, finely wooded. A walled garden ... attached to cottage well stocked with choice fruit trees in full bearing and two orchards and three fields. Gentlemen fond of yachting and fishing would find this a very pleasant situation. There is good mooring ground with three and a half fathoms of water and plentiful fish within stone's throw of cottage. Apply John Mein Esq., Fowey.[44]

An Irish family answered this advertisement, as Patrick Morgan, a widower with five children of twelve and under, was living in the house at the time of the 1851 census. His eldest son, Edward, had been born in France, but the other children had been born in London.[*]

The Morgans may have only been short-term tenants. They were replaced by Captain Charles Henry Searle RN, who died at the house in February 1856, 'after a short and severe illness', aged sixty-six. Following Searle's death the house was again advertised by Mein:

> To let from Michaelmas, a neat cottage residence at Mixtowe, on banks of Fowey River, occupied by representatives of the late Captain Searle. Ground floor: dining and drawing rooms, breakfast parlour, scullery, two kitchens, cellar etc. First floor: four bedrooms, storeroom, closets, atticke and domestic offices, walled garden with fruit trees, two orchards, barn, two acres meadow. Proprietor Captain Mein. Yachts can lie within a few yards, good fishing.[45]

At the time of the following census, in 1861, Captain Mein himself was in residence. Aged seventy-two, he was described as a naval commander on half-pay, born in Fowey. With him were his wife and two unmarried daughters, his sister and a niece, two servants and a local visitor.[†] Mein died in 1870 at Falmouth.

The identity of those living in the house at the time of the census of 1871 is unclear.[‡] In August 1872, however, the house was put up for auction at the Ship Inn in Fowey:

---

[*] Patrick Morgan, forty-seven, widower, annuitant, born in Ireland. His children were Edward, twelve, born in France; Anthony, eight, Joseph, five, and Kate, four, all born in London; also living in the house were Ann Mayrath, thirty-seven, widow, general servant, born in Ireland; and Mary (no surname given), thirteen, general servant, born in Ireland.

[†] Besides John Mein himself, the others were his wife Anne, aged fifty; his sister Catherine, aged seventy-four; his two daughters Rachel and Fanny, twenty-seven and twenty-two; his niece Mary Smith, aged twenty-two; Sophia Lightfoot, a cook, aged twenty-six, and Elizabeth Pearce, a servant, aged nineteen. There was also a visitor, Louisa Kendall, aged fourteen. In 1851, the family had been living at 7 Trafalgar Square, Fowey. Two additional daughters, Anne and Susan, aged seventeen and ten, are listed then.

[‡] Roseblia or Rosiblia Smallridge, aged twenty, and two servants, Elizabeth Canning, twenty-one, and Mary Ann Wall, nineteen. Smallridge was almost certainly not the owner of the house.

Marine villa: early possession. Mr W.F. Congdon will offer for sale by auction, at the Ship Inn, Fowey, on Saturday, 24 August 1872, at three o'clock in the afternoon, a very desirable freehold residence, called Rosebank Villa, replete with domestic offices, and situate on the estuary of the River Fowey, opposite the present terminus of the Lostwithiel and Fowey Railway, four miles from Par station on the Cornwall Railway, and comprising 5 acres, 2 roods and 7 perches of land, which command fine views of the beautiful harbour and scenery. For viewing apply to Captain W.M. Warne, Fowey.

Rosebank was bought, either in 1872 or later in the 1870s, by a London architect, Henry Vulliamy, the son of the well-known architect, Lewis Vulliamy. Henry and his wife, Alice, clearly enjoyed seaside holidays in the West Country, as in their address at the time of the 1891 census was at Littleham, near Exmouth. When Vulliamy died, in 1895, he left his estate to his widow. She had been born as Alice Mary Marston in Brompton in 1855. Her father Robert, a merchant, and mother Isabella were living at 6 Gunter Grove in Chelsea in 1861. In 1871 Alice was living with her mother's sister, Mary Atkinson, at Highgate Lodge in Highgate. After the death of her first husband, she married again, in 1900, becoming Mrs Henry Rainey.[46]

Although he never bought the freehold, and remained a tenant at Rosebank, the house's best-known resident, Alice Rainey's first cousin, Edward Atkinson, seems to have moved to Fowey in 1879, though only a cook and a gardener were there on the night of the census of 1881.[47] Atkinson was also absent on the night of the 1891 census.* Born in 1840, in Hornsey, Middlesex, he was a wealthy bachelor who had inherited money from the family perfumery business. The company had been founded by James Atkinson in Bloomsbury in 1811 before its showroom moved to 24 Old Bond Street. Besides a range of soaps, specialities included Atkinson's

---

    *   On the night of the 1881 census Louisa Bassett, the cook, aged thirty-nine, and Thomas Reath, the gardener, aged thirty, were in the house. At the time of the 1891 census, two of Edward Atkinson's cousins, Louisa and Catherine Marston, aged fifty-one and fifty, Thomas Reath, now forty, and another servant, Bessie Varcoe, aged twenty-seven, were living there. In 1901, Atkinson himself, aged sixty-one, was living there with his two cousins, Thomas Reath, now fifty, Grace Sebire, forty-four, the cook, and two housemaids, Ellen Nicholls and Edith Bunney, aged twenty and fifteen. Finally, in 1911, the year of his death, Atkinson was living there with Catherine Marston, Grace Sebire, the cook, and Ethel Golley, a servant aged twenty-five.

Original Curling Fluid and Atkinson's Vegetable Dye for Grey Hair. The company also imported bear's grease, 'sourced from Russia'. The business was clearly highly profitable.

As was not uncommon with successful nineteenth-century firms, the family beneficiaries in later generations concentrated on leisure rather than business. Atkinson, who had been educated at Highgate, was a keen balloonist and canoeist. After a brief stint working for the family business in Paris, he left its management to his brother. He settled at Rosebank, where two first cousins, first Louisa and then Kate Marston acted as his housekeepers, making many changes to the house. These included adding an eastern wing to Rosebank to house a picture gallery to display his art collection, which included drawings by Turner, a billiard room and a conservatory. A kind and hospitable eccentric, 'Atky' wore a range of idiosyncratic hats imported from Paris, collected mechanical toys and reached the only entrance to his bedroom by a rope ladder.

Atkinson was a passionate sailor, becoming the first commodore of the Fowey Yacht Club between 1894 and 1911. He owned over thirty boats, keeping them in several boathouses at Mixtow. He built the boathouse on Rosebank land at what is now known as Watty's. (William Watty built Atkinson's favourite boat, *Airymouse*, a fifty-eight foot cutter named after the Cornish word for a bat.)[*] Atkinson also built a sizeable boathouse at Tonkin's Quay.

Atkinson drew two literary figures to Mixtow. The first was Arthur Quiller-Couch (1863–1944), a prolific journalist and novelist, born in Bodmin in 1863, who had been familiar with Fowey since his childhood.[48] He married a local girl, Louisa Hicks. Although often away in London and Cambridge, Quiller-Couch spent as much time as he could in Fowey, living at The Haven on the Esplanade and gardening at Prime Cellars, below Hall Walk. 'Q', as he became known, wrote a series of novels, the first of which was *The Astonishing History of Troy Town* (1888), set in Fowey, in which Rosebank is named Kits House and is the house of Mr Fogo, a character based on Atkinson. Quiller-Couch, knighted in 1910 for his public

---

[*] *Airymouse* was launched in July 1894: 'All Fowey and its many visitors seemed afloat on Thursday evening, to witness the launch of a yacht built by Mr Watty after designs by Mr Edwin Brett, for Mr Edward Atkinson of Rosebank, Fowey'. Unfortunately, as 'she dipped in the water with a fall of a few feet she shipped a large quantity of water and all on board were swamped', *Royal Cornwall Gazette*, 12 July 1894.

services, was also a dedicated yachtsman and succeeded Atkinson as the commodore of what became the Royal Fowey Yacht Club.[49]

Atkinson became a close friend of the writer Kenneth Grahame (1859–1932), who first visited Fowey in 1899.[50] Grahame's marriage to Elspeth Thompson, celebrated at the church of St Fimbarrus in Fowey in the same year, was an unhappy one but resulted in the birth of a son, Alastair, known as 'Mouse'. Rather than holidaying with his wife, Grahame preferred to potter around in boats at Fowey, and even went on a lengthy trip to France with Atkinson in 1904. With Elspeth retreating into ill health, Grahame, already a successful author, wrote to 'Mouse' with tales of the riverbank, which featured happy stories of bachelor life and messing about in boats. Many of these letters were written from the Fowey Hotel. *The Wind in the Willows*, which originated from these stories, appeared in 1908 and was hugely successful.[*] As a work of fiction, it is ultimately futile to tie down its characters and location to any one place. Grahame undoubtedly drew on his riverbank experiences at both Cookham in Berkshire, where he had a house, and Fowey. That Atkinson, whose character contained so many of Ratty's attitudes, contributed to the gestation of *The Wind in the Willows* seems beyond doubt.

The Finance Act of 1910, which introduced a new land value tax, made necessary the compilation of another register of land holdings throughout England.[51] The returns of the survey provide the first comprehensive snapshot of ownership in Mixtow since the Tithe Redemption register. The first part of the survey is a record, on Ordnance Survey maps of 1907, of the exact land holdings of individual fields, showing also the houses and outbuildings. The second part consists of the surveyors' field note-books, filled in by hand, listing details about the ownership, occupation, condition and value of individual holdings. The main valuation is of the land, and of the buildings and structures on it, with timber and fruit trees being assessed as separate items.

The survey confirms that Rosebank was not owned by Edward Atkinson, who paid an annual rent of £50 to his cousin, Alice Rainey, who lived in Hove. It was described as a 'detached house, pleasant situation

---

[*] Being the son of a famous children's author did not bring 'Mouse' happiness. While an undergraduate at Oxford, Alastair Grahame committed suicide, on 7 May 1920, by lying on the track of the railway near Port Meadow. Alison Prince, *Kenneth Grahame: An Innocent in the Wild Wood* (London, 1994), pp. 308–15.

but very bad approach. Land rather scattered and mixed with adjoining property'. The house had a dining room, drawing room, two large picture galleries, a kitchen, two pantries, a scullery and a lamp room. It also had five bedrooms, a bathroom and two water closets, as well a greenhouse and summer house. Its boathouse, almost as tall as the house, was well away from it at the furthest point of Mixtow, near Wiseman's Point.

While he did not own Rosebank, or its adjacent cottage (three rooms, dairy, washhouse and coal house), Atkinson had recently acquired the freehold of Mixtow House, and of Mixtow and Polmort Farm, from the Rashleighs, paying £2850 for them together in April 1909.[*] Mixtow House, described as a 'detached house, good situation looking down the harbour – rather awkward for the railway', had two front rooms, plus a kitchen and scullery; two front bedrooms and a dressing room; and two back bedrooms, a boxroom and a water closet. The tenement attached to it had a kitchen and scullery, with a bedroom and water closet above. The house also had a large boathouse, with a workshop over it, as well as two smaller boathouses and a timber store. The land at Polmort is described as 'compact but hilly', while that at Mixtow was 'scattered and mixed with other property'. At Polmort or Polmorland there was only an open shed, sixteen feet tall but in poor condition. At Mixtow Farm, besides a cider-house, yeastinghouse, stable, cattle house and piggery, there were two rooms on the ground floor and three bedrooms above in the cottage.

Dorset Farm, of seventy-three acres, was owned by John Rashleigh, of Trowleigh, Okehampton, but occupied by William Lamb, under a ninety-nine year lease on three lives from 17 January 1859. The farmhouse, where the third William Lamb and his sisters lived in 1911, was twenty-eight feet high and had a sitting room, kitchen, dairy and four bedrooms.[†] The surveyor noted, however, the 'bad approach to the homestead. Interior of house in bad state of repair. Very old'. Lamb did not own Dorset Farm but he did own the freehold of the neighbouring Castle Farm, with its twenty-seven acres. The latter was described as 'Land close to home stead in good heart; land adjoining river and Penpoll Creek thin and very steep'.

---

[*] What had usually been referred to as 'Mixtow and Polmorland Farm' was referred to as 'Mixtow and Polmort Farm' in later times and certainly in the twentieth century.

[†] William John Lamb, the third William Lamb in a row to occupy Dorset Farm, aged fifty-eight but unmarried, was living there in 1911. With him were his sisters Janey, aged fifty, described as a 'housekeeper', and Lizzie, aged forty-five.

The house at Castle Farm, with a kitchen and back kitchen and three bedrooms, was inhabited by a labourer and in poor repair. In 1911 Percy Libby, a farm labourer aged twenty-five, was living there with his wife Elizabeth, aged twenty-four, and their daughter, Gladys, aged two.[52]

The two largest farms, Lombard, occupied by Jane Varcoe and Colin Ferris, and Lombard, Yeate and White Cross, occupied by Herbert Carnall, were both owned by John Bevill Fortescue of Boconnoc. Varcoe and Ferris paid an annual rate of £174 13s. 4d. for their 194 acres (which included the separate holding of Lombard Normansland). In the 1911 census Jane Varcoe, aged sixty-five and born in Polruan, is described as a widow. Living with her nephew were her nephew, John Colin Bennett, aged thirty-three but born in Brompton, Kent, and his wife Mabel, née Ferris, aged twenty-five and born in Pont. There were also four farm hands or servants. Herbert Carnall paid £128 8s. 3d. annually for his 109 acres at Yeate. Carnall also occupied the smaller Mixtow and Polmart Farm, of 35 acres, the freehold of which had recently been acquired by Edward Atkinson from John Rashleigh, paying a rent of £50 a year. In 1911 Carnall, aged forty-six, was living there with his wife, Catherine, aged forty-two, their son Richard, aged nineteen, and two servants.

Both main farms had many additional outbuildings, twenty in the case of Lombard and twelve at Yeate, which also had two cottages. The only general description is of South Lombard, the house, with its small farm: 'Interior of house in bad repair. The fields adjoining Penpoll Creek are very steep and are in very bad condition some of them growing nothing but bracken, thorns and thistles and have apparently not been stocked for years. Remainder of farm in fairly good heart'. The farmhouse at Lombard had a sitting room, two kitchens and a back kitchen, a dairy, a washhouse, two staircases and five bedrooms. The farmhouse at Yeate had three sitting rooms, a kitchen, a dairy, a washhouse and six bedrooms.

Four additional houses are described as 'Lombard', besides the farmhouse, in the 1911 census return. One, on the ancient Butter's Tenement and later known as Bunt's Cottage, was occupied by John Bunt, a farm labourer aged forty-six, his wife, Mary, aged thirty-four, and their two sons, William, eleven, and Mary, four. Thomas Reath, the long-term gardener at Rosebank, aged sixty-one, was living by himself in the cottage next door. In the cottage nearest to Lombard Farm, William Langmaid, a carpenter aged forty-one, was living with his wife, Catherine; their two children, Lawson, aged fourteen, and Vida, aged thirteen; and their niece,

Iris Bray, aged one. Finally, at South Lombard, George Harris, a farmer from Braddock aged sixty-nine, was living with his wife, Anna, also sixty-nine, who had been born in Galway.

The gross sale values of the properties were calculated as Mixtow House £723; Rosebank £1360; Mixtow and Polmort £1414; Castle Farm £1718; Dorset Farm £1475; Lombard, Yeate and Whitecross £3302; and Lombard £4078. The most valuable buildings and structures were Rosebank at £1100 and Mixtow House at £595, making up a large percentage of the value of these two properties as a whole. The buildings at the main farms were valued at £320 at Dorset, £560 at Lombard and £560 at Yeate. The buildings at Mixtow and Polmort were worth £500, while those at Castle, where the house was lived in by a labourer, were valued at only £216. The value of timber and fruit make up only a small part of the valuations. The most valuable timber was £30 at Yeate and the most valuable fruit was £25 at Dorset.

Edward Atkinson's end was sad but fitting. Setting out for Looe on the evening of 9 September 1911 in an eighteen-foot sailing boat, the *Gyotis*, with Quiller-Couch's son Bevil, the two men sheltered off Lantic Bay overnight.[53] In the morning, after deciding to work back towards Fowey, the boat was struck by a gust of wind and started filling with water. Unfortunately, the boat's supposedly watertight air tanks were faulty. Swimming to the shore from 500 yards, Bevil managed to land; but the weaker Atkinson could not get through the breakers and drowned, despite Bevil's best efforts. An inquest was held at Mixtow House before a funeral at Lanteglos parish church. Thirty boats made up a funeral cortège to the end of Pont Creek, from where the coffin was carried up to the church.

A week later, Kenneth Grahame wrote to a mutual friend:

I loved Atky – in perhaps a selfish way first of all because his special 'passions' appealed to me – boats, Bohemianism, Burgundy, tramps, travel, books and pictures ... Again and again, in imagination, I get my boat at Whitehouse Steps and scull up river by the grey old sea wall, under the screaming gulls, past the tall Russian and Norwegian ships at their moorings, and so into Mixtow Pill, and ship my oars at the little stone pier, and find Atky waiting on the steps, thin, in blue serge, with his Elizabethan head; and stroll up the pathway you know, to the little house above it, and he talking all the time and always some fresh whimsicality.[54]

1. Fowey Harbour in 1540. Part of a map of the defences of the south coast from Land's End to Exeter. Mixtow, above Pendennick (Bodinnick), where a ferry boat is crossing, is shown as equal in size to Pont, Penpoll and Lerryn creeks. British Library, Cotton MS Augustus I, i. (*British Library*)

2. Fowey in the 1880s. (*Samuel Sheppard*)

3. Bodinnick in the 1880s, before the new road up to Whitecross, showing the boatyard there at work. (*Samuel Sheppard*)

4. The earliest photograph of Mixtow, showing the quay at high tide.
(*Paul Richards*)

5. Mixtow in the 1880s. Left to right, Watty's boathouse and wood stores, ships
hauled up on Mixtow beach, Mixtow Quay, Mixtow Farm and Mixtow House.
(*Paul Richards*)

6. Caffa Mill Pill, with the railway running beside it but before it was filled in and turned into a car park. The Bodinnick Ferry is crossing to its old slipway. (*Martin Sheppard*)

7. An early view of Mixtow Docks with Mixtow Pill behind. (*Paul Richards*)

8. The opening of the Great Western Railway's No. 8 Jetty, Fowey Docks, on 27 September 1923. (*Paul Richards*)

9. Loading at No. 7 Jetty, with Watty's boathouse and Flagstaff Cottage behind. Mixtow Quay and Pill to the right. (*Paul Richards*)

10. US Marines drinking at the Safe Harbour, 1944. (*Paul Richards*)

11. American landing craft leaving Fowey Harbour through its boom, 1944. (*Paul Richards*)

12, 13 and 14. Three views of US Navy men at Mixtow, 1944.
(*Robert Bond and Isabel Pickering*)

15. Mixtow Pill and Kits House in 1963. (*Hilary Severn*)

16. View from near the end of Mixtow Pill looking across at Kits House.
(*Paul Richards*)

17. The Varco brothers, George, Robert and Charles, leading retailers in Fowey. Robert Varco (1879–1961), centre, the landlord of the Lugger and a vintner, owned much of Mixtow between the wars. A prominent local figure, he was a County Councillor and Chairman of the Governors of Fowey Grammar School.
(*Paul Richards*)

18. Captain John Mein RN, the naval surgeon who built Rosebank (subsequently Kits House) in the 1830s. (*Martin Sheppard*)

19. Kenneth Grahame, the author of *The Wind in the Willows* and close friend of Edward Atkinson. (*Private Collection*)

20. Edward Atkinson, the first Commodore of the Royal Fowey Yacht Club. (*Royal Fowey Yacht Club*)

21. Charles Varcoe, who succeeded his father, also Charles Varcoe, at Lombard Farm. (*Wendy Parfitt*)

22. Archie and Carrie Tippett (back row, second and third from the left), who farmed Mixtow Farm between the wars. (*Betty Davies*)

23. A paying guest at Mixtow Farm enjoys milking a cow. (*Betty Davies*)

SOUTH CORNWALL

FOWEY RIVER HARBOURSIDE PROPERTY

of great charm in an unrivalled situation with about 1,000ft. of
tidal frontage and private quay

MIXTOW PILL ESTATE
Lanteglos-by-Fowey

FOR SALE BY AUCTION
IN SEVEN LOTS ON

1st April, 1963

(unless previously sold privately as a complete estate)

MAY, WHETTER & GROSE
Auctioneers and Surveyors

CORNUBIA HALL
FAR
CORNWALL

TREGONISSEY HOUSE
ST. AUSTELL
CORNWALL

24. The auction brochure for the sale of the Mixtow Pill Estate. (*John Pollard*)

25. Leslie Clifford Brown.
(*Penny Tuck*)

26. Pat Brown with her niece, Penny Smart,
and daughter Lucil. (*Penny Tuck*)

27. Hilary Saxton's wedding to Roy Severn, Bristol, 1957. Frank and Freda Saxton
are at the end on the left; Bob Saxton is to the right of the bride. (*Hilary Severn*)

28. Fowey Docks under construction, 1972, looking across to Mixtow. (*Imerys*)

29. The storage linhay nearing completion, 1972. (*Imerys*)

30. Stella and Bill Poole.
(*Lucy Sheppard*)

31. Lucy, Henry and Geoffrey Poole. (*Lucy Sheppard*)

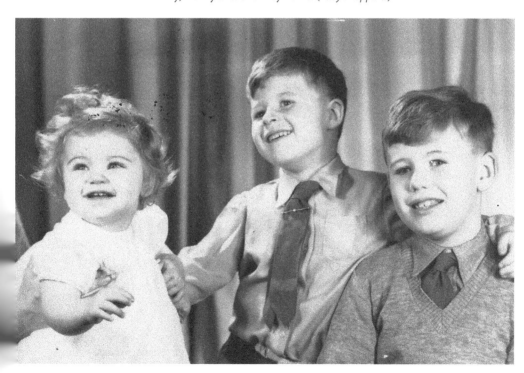

32. A ship entering Mixtow Pool. (*Catherine Turbett*)

33. Penmarlam Boat Park. (*Catherine Turbett*)

Grahame even considered buying the house, but nothing came of this: 'We have been up to Rosebank – a sad sight rather, with its empty rooms and bare walls ... The place is for sale, not to be let, and I don't think it will sell in a hurry – it's not everybody's home'.[55]

Atkinson's will divided his estate between two of his first cousins, Catherine Isabel Marston, who had been living with him at Rosebank, and Alice Mary Rainey.[56] While he left the residue of his estate to Catherine Marston, he left Mixtow House, including Mixtow and Polmort farm, to Alice Rainey, who already owned Rosebank. He also left Alice Rainey 'any such pictures, prints, jewellery, furniture or other of my personal effects as she may select to the total value of five hundred pounds'. What became of his art collection, including the drawings by Turner, is unclear. While his gross estate was valued at £25,300 6s. 6d., its net value was only £11,978 13s. 2d. His will specifically mentions a loan of £1000, dating from 1909, needing to be repaid to Alice Rainey in connection with the purchase of Mixtow House and Farm.

Although twice married, Alice Rainey, like her cousin, Edward Atkinson, had no children. Within a few years, she had disposed of both Mixtow and Rosebank. In 1915 she sold Mixtow House and farmland on the north bank of Mixtow Pill to Robert Varco of Fowey for £1400.[57] After many centuries of being held together, as Mixtow and Polmort Farm, she sold the farmland on the other side of Mixtow Pill to John Bevill Fortescue of Boconnoc for £700 in the same year.[58]

The new owner of Mixtow House, and of the farm next to it, was Robert Varco, one of three Varco brothers. All were leading shopkeepers in Fowey. Robert, who had been born in 1879, was the proprietor of Varco's Wine and Spirit Store in Fore Street, next to the Lugger, which he also owned. His brother Charles was a silversmith, jeweller, clockmaker, watch-repairer and optician, also in Fore Street, while George ran the main grocers shop in Fowey, on the corner of the Esplanade and West Street.* The businesses were all successful, enabling George Varco to buy Carnethic House, one of the largest houses in Fowey, and Robert to buy property in Mixtow as an investment. Robert and his wife, Edith, had three children, Henry, Marion and Phyllis. While Henry became the bank manager of Lloyds in Launceston, his sister Marion Willcox was living

---

* The family came originally from Lanlivery. Robert Varco's grandfather, also Robert, was a carpenter who acquired the Lugger, which was subsequently owned by his son George, the father of Charles, George and Robert.

in 1961 at Crayford Manor House in Crayford, Kent. Robert Varco was a prominent local figure in Fowey, becoming Chairman of the Governors of Fowey Grammar School and a County Councillor.

Edward Atkinson, with his large collection of boats, had built a number of boathouses in Mixtow. The grandest of these, with a sail loft above it, was the late Victorian boathouse near to Wiseman's Point.* (This was on the site of the earlier boathouse and fish cellar belonging to John Mein.) Atkinson's boat-builder and repairer was Archie Watty, who lived in a cottage built next to the boathouse. Sadly, Watty and his wife, Millicent, lost a baby there from pneumonia.† Atkinson was so upset that he added an additional story to the cottage to make life easier for the Wattys, who lived there until after the Second World War.

Archie Watty came from a boat-building family in Fowey, where Watty's was a well-known boat-building yard. A Cornishman of his time, Watty was very short and had a high-pitched voice. His wife, who wore plaits and ringlets, was much taller than he was. She was always busy around the house and seldom seemed to come out of it. Watty usually wore an old-fashioned chauffeur's uniform: black with a peaked cap with a white top (starched white every day). He was very knowledgeable about anything to do with the water, but wouldn't usually give out information. Occasionally, he might issue hints about where to fish. Watty built all sorts of boats, including rowing boats, as well as the first Troy class sailing boat. He built his own 18' to 20' fishing boat.

Next to his cottage, Watty had a timber store. Between the wars, Watty's timber store was replaced by two bungalows, known as No. 1 and No. 2. The holes for the beams used by Watty to support the racks on which he stored wood can still be seen in the wall behind the bunga-lows. Roger and Margery King, from Surrey, came on honeymoon to Fowey in 1936 and stayed at the Ferryside Hotel, next to the old slipway.[59] There they met a much older couple, from the same village in Surrey, who

---

* Watty's boathouse still has the original glass at the front. It once had a concrete slipway and a wooden extension, traces of which can still be seen.

† Archie Watty, the son of the boat builder William Watty and his wife, Emma, had been born in 1875. In 1911 he and his wife, Millicent, were living at 138 Esplanade in Fowey, with their daughter Mavis and a servant. He is described as a yacht-builder and as an employer. He died in St Austell in 1949.

suggested a joint river trip. Together they went to see No. 2. The elderly couple were considering renting it, but decided against the idea. The Kings, having seen it by chance, rented it themselves from Robert Varco. They used to drive down every weekend in a Ford 8, a journey that often took nine hours. The Kings and their two sons, Simon and Richard, subsequently spent many weekends and as well as holidays at Mixtow.[60]

Rosebank, which was renamed Kits House at this time, changed hands several times between Edward Atkinson's death and the outbreak of the Second World War. It was sold by Alice Rainey to Frank Kilpatrick, of 7 Brandon Road, Southsea, a tar distiller, for £1500 in 1919. Then Kilpatrick, now of Kirkstall, Alverstoke, Hampshire, sold it in 1928 for £2250 to Vivian Thomas, of 3 Tolcarne Road, Newquay. Thomas sold it on the following month, for £2750, to Hubert Bower, of Higher Cotley, Dunsford, near Exeter. Bower, in turn, sold it on eighteen months later to Winifred Hart of the Hackbridge Hotel, Surrey, for £2250, a diminution in price perhaps reflecting the downturn after the 1929 Wall Street crash. Following her marriage to Lieutenant-Colonel Hugh Davies, in March 1940, when she moved to Carlyon Bay, Winifred Davies sold Rosebank to William Tapley, of Washington, Redbridge, Southampton, for £2000.

During the 1930s, a bungalow had been built to the east of Rosebank. It seems to have been already in place when it was sold by Winifred Hart to Ella Bayly, on 20 October 1931, for £300. Nothing is now visible of this bungalow, which burnt down on 3 June 1953.

Alice Rainey died in London in 1930. Under her will she left the large boathouse next to Mixtow House, which she had kept for herself when she sold off Mixtow House and Rosebank, and £3000 to her solicitor, Ernest Kite, of 2 Dean's Yard, The Sanctuary, Westminster:

And to Ernest Acton Kite (in recognition of many kindnesses shown by him to me and the various members of my family for many years and often unpaid work; he indeed having been our guide, philosopher and friend) the sum of three thousand pounds.

And I also give to the said Ernest Acton Kite my piece of freehold land with the boathouse thereon at Mixtow, Lanteglos-by-Fowey, called 'Tonkin's Quay', and such of my furniture, plate, books and personal effects as he may select.

This transaction explains how the boathouse, which was subsequently turned into Tonkins Quay House, became separated from Mixtow House.

As well as various legacies to family members, Alice Rainey left a small house in Fowey itself to its occupier: 'I give my household dwelling house at Fowey now in the occupation of Nicholas Steggell and the sum of fifty pounds to the said Nicholas Steggell'. The residue of her estate was divided between King's College Hospital, Denmark Hill, and St Thomas's Hospital.[61]

For nine years after Alice Rainey's death, Mixtow remained a quiet backwater. Then, in September 1939, all changed. With the outbreak of war, the south coast of Cornwall became part of the front line in the war against Hitler.

3

Mixtow at War

FOWEY HAD SENT ships and sailors to war since the middle ages.
It provided the *Francis of Foy* to meet the Armada and seamen for
Nelson's navy. Mixtow itself also attracted a number of retired naval
officers as residents, including John Mein and Henry Searle, as well as the
master mariner, Joseph Sloggett.[1]

The First World War, which broke out in August 1914, led to the deaths
of forty-two Fowey men and twenty-three from Lanteglos, mostly serving
in the army in France and Belgium.[2] The war also brought to an end a
boom in the china clay trade, which had produced a record 860,649 tons
in 1912, three-quarters of which was exported to America and Europe,
and half of which was shipped via Fowey. Cut off from markets by the
war and by a shortage of shipping, and with large amounts of unsold
clay in stock, production fell to 463,632 tons by 1917. All local industries,
including farming, were affected by a lack of manpower due to recruit-
ment to the armed forces.[3] Fishing was particularly hard hit, as many
young fishermen, as reservists, were quickly called up into the Navy.[4]

Mixtow's experience of the Second World War echoed that of Fowey.
Although not a major German target such as Plymouth, or even Falmouth,
Fowey's position on a deep-water estuary gave it strategic significance
as a port and as an obvious base for smaller navy ships.[5] From early in
the war the entrance to Fowey Harbour was protected by a controlled

minefield, with a firing point inside St Catherine's Castle. Two six-inch guns also protected the harbour mouth. Reviving a long-abandoned mode of defence, a boom made of large steel buoys with a steel-mesh net beneath was stretched between Polruan and the old Fowey blockhouse. A tubular defence barrier blocked the entrance to Readymoney Cove.[6] Barrage balloons also were put up to deter enemy aircraft.

Many of the buildings in and around Fowey were commandeered for military use.[7] The Navy, which played the leading role in Fowey during the war, took over the Fowey Hotel and the Town Quay. On the east side of the harbour, the Navy requisitioned Ferryside and the Ferry Inn at Bodinnick, and Kits House and Mixtow House at Mixtow, as accommodation for officers. Other branches of the services took over other parts of Fowey, with the Royal Artillery establishing itself at Point Neptune. A small RAF unit was based at Nos 8 and 10 Station Road. The Town Hall was used for entertainment and the British Legion Club as a NAAFI store.[8] Further afield, in the run-up to D-Day, the Americans took over Boconnoc House and used it as an ammunition dump.

The earliest change at Mixtow was in 1941, when the harbour master put in hand the building of a slipway at Mixtow Quay, to allow naval ratings to land at low tide. Built between April and June that year at a cost of £600, the work was paid for by the Admiralty. On 28 May the log book of the Harbour Commission read: 'The commissioners' men have constructed a causeway for naval parties to land at Mixtow adjoining the quay. This is nearly complete only waiting a favourable tide to place the top in position. This is quite an addition to the landing places of the port, there being three feet of water available at the lowest tide'.[9]

During the early years of the war a great variety of ships were based in the harbour or were regular visitors to it. While no major warships used Fowey, a wide range of smaller ships, including minesweepers, gun-boats, salvage ships and landing craft, filled the harbour. Many of the ships were no more than converted trawlers and drifters, fitted with guns. Z boats, previously motor yachts belonging to the wealthy, were used as coastal patrol vessels. Motor Gun Boats (MGBs) were also stationed at Fowey. Entrance and exit to the harbour was strictly controlled by the Resident Naval Officers, Captain Perryman (1940–42) and Commander Newcombe (1942–45). Fowey was the gathering point for ships from Charlestown and Par assembling as convoys.[10]

This naval activity made the town the target for a number of German bombs between May 1940 and August 1942. Mixtow itself was not bombed, offering little in the way of a target, but a number of bombs and mines fell nearby in the river. On 3 April 1941 a German explosive float was neutralised just off Mixtow by the Royal Naval Bomb and Mine Disposal Squad. Bodinnick was hit on 3 April and again on 15 July 1941, when Sir Arthur Quiller-Couch was fortunate to escape injury while working in his garden at Prime Cellars, on the east side of the harbour, as four high explosive bombs fell on Hall Walk. The Boys School at Polruan was wrecked in another raid.[11] Lerryn attracted five bombs on 25 February and one on 5 July 1941. St Winnow, perhaps because of its position near to the end of the estuary, suffered four bomb attacks in 1941, while Golant was machine-gunned in August 1942. Mostly, the attacks were by single planes, returning from Falmouth or overshooting Plymouth, and there was limited damage.[12]

Much more harm might have been done by a lucky hit or by a dedicated raid. Two 250,000 gallon oil storage tanks were built to supply naval ships behind Nos 1 and 2 Jetties of the docks above Fowey. A second conspicuous target was presented by the supplies of ammunition and explosives shipped through the port. These were stockpiled in large quantities in Cornish clay pits, centred around Bugle. They were transported down to Fowey Docks by train or lorry and then shipped to the British Expeditionary Force, before the Fall of France; and, later in the war, to the British and American forces in France on D-Day and afterwards.

Because of its importance in the shipping of explosives, the line from Lostwithiel to Fowey was shut from 1 January to 9 February 1940 and again from 24 August to 3 October 1942; over D-Day it was shut from 2 May to 2 October 1944. The track was fenced off from Fowey Station as far as Golant and guarded by sentries. Dockers were searched on entering the docks to check that they had no matches on them. To reduce the risk of keeping explosives in one place, two railway sidings were dug out at Woodgate Pill, between Fowey and Lostwithiel, where ammunition wagons could wait until the docks were ready for them.[13]

The RAF unit based in Fowey was involved in towing targets resembling U-boats out to sea to help train pilots. One of its less successful efforts ended up at Mixtow:

> In 1942 the target used originally was the Orepesa float, made from a minesweeping float. It could be made to dive by controlling the towing cables and a fluorescent dye was released when it submerged. It seems, however, that something larger and more like a U-boat was wanted

and in 1943 a large, heavy target known as Submersible Target I was towed back, with difficulty, from Devonport. Only three knots could be made as the target swerved about on its tow line. An old Royal Navy steamer, the *Golden Miller*, tried to tow it, with little more success. It was intended that someone should be inside and signal the hits! This was never put to the test. The target was not a success and was towed upriver and left at high tide near Mixtow.[14]

Submersible Target II, which included a replica conning tower and periscope, but no human observer, fortunately proved much more successful.

The desperate need to feed the nation during the Battle of the Atlantic focused government attention on farm production. The result was a survey of farms across the country, with a series of questionnaires sent out to all farmers.[15] The responses to the questionnaires provide a snapshot of ownership, tenancy, livestock and crops at Mixtow in 1941. The maps drawn up to go with the survey show exactly which fields were held at that time by the six principal farmers.

Richard Carnall had held Yeate Farm for eighteen years and paid a rental of £170.[16] Lombard was divided into two parts, one farmed by John Ferris, established there for thirty-seven years, at a rent of £153; and a smaller part by his son, Thomas Ferris, there only since 1938, at £30. John Girdlestone had leased fifty acres of Dorset Farm for twenty-one years. He had rented another twenty acres for ten years from Mr Steed of Pont. He also rented two meadows for summer grazing from William Tapley of Mixtow House.[17] Mary Libby, and her son Sydney, of Castle had held the farm of six and a half years at a rent of £95. Ernest Motton paid a rent of £46 for Mixtow Farm, which he had held for only a year and a half.

Most of the farms were worked by their owners or tenants, but there were two labourers on Yeate and one on Dorset. John Ferris had two of his sons working on Lombard, while Mary Libby and her son farmed Castle. Dorset, Lombard and Yeate each had a tractor, but there were still twelve working horses on the farms. All the farms combined crop and animal farming, though the government was urging farmers to turn more of their fields over to growing crops. The returns show that sixty-two acres out of a total of 411 on the six farms had been converted in this way during 1940 and the first half of 1941. Out of this total acreage, however, eighty-two acres are described on the returns as 'Rough Grazing', which it would have been difficult to cultivate.

Farming at Mixtow in 1941

Crops (Acres)	Castle	Dorset	Lombard* (a)	(b)	Mixtow	Yeate
Wheat	3		8			10
Barley	3		23			3
Oats	3	8	16		1	8
Mixed Corn	6	8	3	7		12
Potatoes	1	3	3		1	2
Turnips	1	1	4		1	2
Mangolds	1	1	1			
Kale	1	1	1		1	2
Rape			4			
Vetches		3				
Orchards		3		1		2
Clover	8	21	15	13		43
Grass	31	16	46		9	34
Other		3	2	2	4	1
Total	58	68	126	23	17	119
Rough	10	25	23	12	6	6
Live Stock						
Cows	25	23	31	15	6	37
Sheep	20		42			44
Pigs	17	7	56		1	26
Poultry	16	50	30		63	59
Horses	3	3	2		1	3

---

* At Lombard John Ferris's return is marked (a) and that of his son, Thomas, as (b).

In common with other ports along the south coast of England, Fowey
had an important role to play in the preparations for and launch of
D-Day. Well before that, the Admiralty had been considering whether
and where to install grids for the repair of landing craft. A naval report
dated 24 December 1942, marked 'Most Secret', analysed seven possible
sites for repair grids in Fowey Harbour.* Mixtow Pill itself was rejected:
'Surveys have been made but sites are *not* considered suitable owing the
great depth of mud over these areas'. Mixtow Quay and the beach above
it, however, attracted two possible schemes:

> Scheme A. This scheme provides for one broadside grid for LCTs
> [Landing Craft Tanks] and six bow-on grids for LCMs [Landing Craft
> Mechanized]. An access road is available. Sites suitable for work-
> shop and store are shown on an adjoining quay. (All as shown on SCE
> Drawings Nos 01246/42 and 01247/42.)† The estimated approximate
> cost for LCT grid is £3750 and for LCM grid £1650. (This excludes all
> costs of buildings etc.)

> Scheme B. This is an alternative proposal to Scheme A, but shows a
> continuous bow-on grid for LCMs, with additional road access at back.
> (All shown on SCE Drawing No. 01297/42.) The estimated approxi-
> mate cost of the LCT grid is £3750 and for the continuous LCM grid,
> including new road acess £2200. (This excludes all costs of buildings.)

Scheme B, for the use of smaller craft, was considered suitable by the
Admiral of the Fleet:

---

* The correspondence about these plans is in the National Archives, ADM
1/13198. The other sites examined were north of Wiseman's Point ('unsuitable');
Wiseman's Stone Beach ('no road access'); opposite Jetty No. 4 ('no access'); Caffa Mill
('not considered very suitable on account of the mud'); and Pont Pill, near Brazen
Island ('can be approached by beach from the Brazen Island Company's Works'). The
last was considered the best option for larger landing craft: Brazen Island is 'capable
of undertaking all hull work necessary for LCT, and this slip can be used for the
largest types of LCT'.

† Copies of these drawings, and those for all the other suggested schemes,
together with a location map showing the position of the sites in Fowey Harbour,
are in ADM 1/13198. This also shows the area of Mixtow commandeered by the Navy.

There is no suitable site for a small craft slip with a turntable or traverses and it is therefore proposed to meet the requirements of LCM and LCA by the provision of a grid to berth up to six craft at Site 3, as shown on Scheme B with SCE drawing No. 01297/42, with two Nissen huts on the Mixtow Quay to provide the necessary facilities for the work by flotilla personnel. This scheme provides means for attending and securing the craft on the grid at high tide and access to the craft at all times by planks led from the access road to the top grid pillar and planks laid and secured to the pillars as required.

It was not, however, implemented: 'As Fowey is not scheduled as an assault port, it is possible that naval maintenance personnel will not be available at this port during assault and build-up, in which case the LCT grid at Site 3 would be of little use'.

In the end, Mixtow was used as a repair base not for the Royal Navy but for the US Navy. Towards the end of 1943, Fowey became the scene of hectic activity, with the beginnings of an influx of a sizeable number of US troops. At its height, there was a thousand-man camp, in Quonset huts, for the Americans at Windmill Field and another camp for five hundred men at Green Lane, with a smaller one at Mixtow. The Americans took over Fowey Hall, established a store depot in the donkey field at Lamb's Barn Garage, and used Carnethic House as a hospital. Officers were quartered at the St Catherine's Hotel; and the Greenbank Hotel became a US Hospital Training School.[18]

According to a Royal Air Force man:

Fowey streets were soon full of US Navy men and a good lot of men they were. We RAF could visit their canteen, which was in the main street near the old cinema. They all made us welcome, plenty of 'fags' etc. I don't remember any trouble with our forces and the Yanks. We also used to visit the base at Mixtow and have dinner with them. They called it 'chow'.[19]

By the end of May, 'the harbour was so full of vessels we said you could walk from Fowey to Polruan without getting your feet wet, by stepping from one vessel to another'.[20]

Mixtow had a specific role in the preparations for D-Day, as the base for repairing the landing-craft being made ready for the invasion. In January

1944 the 29th Construction Battalion built two Quonset huts behind the
quay, one measuring 20 feet x 40 feet and the other 40 feet by 100 feet.
Under the command of Lieutenant W.J. Cabuisce USN, these housed
workshops for electricians, machinists, carpenters and fitters, as well as a
supply store. Originally, Cabuisce had only three officers and thirty men
at Mixtow, but the size of the unit grew rapidly with the increase in the
number of landing craft in the harbour to seventy-nine. At its peak, the
unit consisted of around 125 men.[21]

According to one of the Americans stationed at what was known as the
US Navy Advanced Amphibious Training Sub Base:

My friend, Joseph Kayata and I berthed in the one-storey small room
on the right as you view the house from the river.* In a corner of the
room a masonry structure supported an iron pot and space for a fire.
One evening we heated a slab of bacon sent from home. That room
was lost to remodeling by 1970. Mr and Mrs Ernest Motton owned
the building on the left, next to Mixtow, and I traded with them – one
cigarette for one egg.

The two officers at Mixtow, Lieutenant George DeGuise and chief
warrant officer Glen Baysden, lived in a trailer which also served as an
office. There were four Quonset workshops there; an MOM shop,[22] an
electric shop ... ship fitter or carpentry. Kits House had berthing and a
kitchen where we had our meals. There were about fifty of us. Another
two-storey building between Mixtow and Kits had berthing and lavatories and a shower stall.[23] Water was heated for this in a small pot-belly
stove. We had two petrol-fuelled American generators for electricity
– 'Chappy' Chapman was their caretaker. One day we found we were
to have real eggs for breakfast. But the eggs had been in storage a long
time; we could taste the storage room! I was the petrol can filler and
carrier to a LCVP [Landing Craft Vehicle Personnel] which took five
first class petty officers to Brazen Island Patent Slipway, where they did
the electric welding on LCT 200s. British employees measured, fitted,
cut all the reinforcing metal plates to make her worthy for a trip to
Normandy. On occasions LCTs would tie up at the quay for service and
repair. They also anchored with their bows jammed close to the river

* Three photos exist of US Navy sailors at Mixtow House, which is being
described here. I am most grateful to Isabel Pickering for sending me copies of these
and Robert Bond's memories of his stay at Mixtow.

bank at high tide and received observation and care of hull, rudder, props and the skin while hung up on the river bank at low tide.[24]

The landing craft needed their engines changing every thousand hours. Usually four landing craft were being repaired at any one time.[*] The smaller landing craft were lifted out of the water onto Mixtow Quay. Larger ones were moored at iron rings on the adjacent beach. Not all the activities of the landing craft were warlike: 'Girls were brought back from dances in Fowey by landing craft, which came right up on the beach before lowering the bow door to let the girls off'.[25] The Americans also taught the local girls to jitterbug.[26]

In order to protect the growing armada of boats in the harbour, and beyond Wiseman's Point, a gun emplacement was sited overlooking Wiseman's, reached by a track from Mixtow Quay.[27] Two anti-aircraft guns were placed in fields at South Torfrey Farm, above Golant.

The Americans, to allow the movement of their large trucks and heavy equipment but to the benefit of Mixtow after the war, also upgraded the local roads. They widened the road up from the Bodinnick ferry to Whitecross, and the lane leading down to Mixtow from Whitecross, to allow their use by heavy trucks, building a road between Castle and Dorset farms for the first time. This gave much better access to the quay at Mixtow, which had previously only been reachable via the end of Mixtow Pill.[†]

With the build-up to D-Day, the amount of ammunition and explosives passing through the harbour again increased:

fifty per cent or more of the ammunition shipped out for use in the D-Day landings came from Fowey. Large barges which were

---

[*]   Vivian Sandy, then at Fowey Grammar School and crossing the harbour twice every day, recalls the large bow waves made by landing craft.

[†]   Because of the narrowness of the lane leading from the end of the pill to Mixtow House, the Americans initially brought in materials along the beach, where there are still signs of a roadway. At one time the road between Bodinnick and Looe turned sharp right to Pelynt a couple of miles after Highway. The main route to Plymouth from Mixtow was via the Torpoint Ferry; almost no one went via Saltash (where the bridge across the Tamar was only opened in 1961). Before 1939 many of the local roads were little better than tracks, being also blocked by farm gates requiring opening and shutting. Information from Richard and Maggie Davies, Madge Norman and Henry Poole.

prefabricated were loaded with ammunition. The parts for these barges were carried here by ship and welded together on arrival at Fowey.[28]

Just before D-Day, a complete clampdown on the movement was enforced, with troops confined to their camps or on board their ships. Finally, 'Titch' Wellington saw them leave:

> From the upstairs window of my house in Daglands Road I had a full view of the build-up in the harbour. I saw it fill up with LSTs [Landing Ship Tanks], LCTs etc, with troops on deck little realising what it meant. Then on Tuesday 6 June, we woke up to find the harbour completely empty and we heard that D-Day had begun.[29]

The flotilla which sailed from Fowey consisted of eight Landing Ship Tanks, thirteen Landing Craft Infantry (Large), five rhino barges (for the actual landing on the beach), five tugs and one repair barge, carrying American troops to Omaha Beach, though not landing in the first wave.[30] It joined up with other units of the enormous invasion fleet, including those from Plymouth, before crossing the Channel.

According to Mavis Cocks,

> What I remember is the absolute stillness of everything. In a way we had suffered a small invasion of our own, when all those Americans came over, and quite a large number were in billets in and around Fowey ... We were also now used to the American drawl and accent, and to seeing large numbers of these friendly, noisy men being around ... So, the harbour was full of busy activity one day, and the next all gone and everything so still![31]

Although Fowey was active in shipping explosives and ammunition after D-Day, and was still full of service personnel, its main part in the war was over. At the end of the war, after celebrating VE Day in style, the requisitioned buildings were slowly handed back to their civilian owners.[32] The boathouse between Mixtow House and Mixtow Farm had been badly damaged during the US Navy's occupation, as had the quay itself. After the war, the Quonset huts were demolished and all the machinery and other equipment used in the repair of the landing craft was taken, fittingly by landing craft, out to sea and dumped.[33]

4

The Docks

F ROM ITS NORTH bank, Mixtow has a fine view down the harbour
towards Fowey and Polruan. To the south east is an unbroken line
of trees, other than the New Quay near Bodinnick. On the west bank of
the River Fowey, however, directly opposite the mouth of Mixtow Pill
and impossible to ignore, is a line of docks. Behind its cranes, hoists and
conveyor belts, which stretch from Caffa Mill to Upper Carne Point, rises
a large shed, crowned by the trees of Colvithick Wood. Lorries service
the ships moored at the docks; and, at its most northerly point, there
is a freight train terminal. Although these docks are not physically part
of Mixtow, being separated from it by the river, they have been part of
Mixtow's history over the last one hundred and fifty years.

Fowey is a deep-water port, on an estuary well protected from the
weather, but until the nineteenth century its trade was restricted to
the town's own quays and to those of Polruan, on the other side of the
harbour mouth. These quays and the warehouses behind them, nearly all
small-scale and privately owned, were crammed together by the steep rise
in the land on all sides of the harbour. Although Fowey had been a major
port in the middle ages and Tudor times, competition from Plymouth and
Falmouth, and the concentration of commerce and industry in the east
and north of England, had led to a dwindling of its trade by the end of
the eighteenth century. The export of pilchards, its long-term staple, was

hard hit by a tax on salt and by the loss of European outlets during the
prolonged wars with France.

Already in 1759, a visitor noted Fowey's decline:

> This town supports itself by its fishery, and trade to Norway for deals,
> much depopulated ... so that they complain'd it had not left them above
> one man to seven women. A poor mean place; its harbour defended by
> four batteries with twenty-one guns, which have no gunner, ammu-
> nition or touch-hole ... Town rich in nothing but two members of
> Parliament.[1]

During the eighteenth century, when ships were still responsible for the
arrival of most goods brought from a distance, including coal, limestone and
timber, Fowey and the area around it was noted as a centre of smuggling.[2]
A reaction to heavy government duties on a range of goods, including the
excise on salt and spirits, smuggling was not regarded as reprehensible by
most Cornishmen, who willingly bought the cheaper goods made available
by this evasion of tax. A thriving connection was set up between Fowey
and suppliers in Guernsey and, later, St-Malo. The scale of the 'Trade', as it
was known, encouraged the building of sloops in Fowey. At around sixty
tons, these were fast, cheap and manoeuvrable. Easy to beach for loading
and unloading, they were ideally suited to their business. The rewards of
smuggling increased due to high levels of taxation during the Napoleonic
Wars, despite an active campaign by Revenue officers to suppress it. Many
Fowey men made a living from the sea, whether in the Royal Navy or as
smugglers, ship-builders and repairers, fishermen or as the crews of ships
engaged in national and international trade.

Although the tin-mining industry was priced out by foreign competition, Fowey's commercial decline was reversed by the growth of three
Cornish industries, first copper, then iron and then china clay.[3] All three
needed large-scale shipping facilities to supply their markets. The industrialist Joseph Treffry hoped that Fowey could be made into a large and
thriving port, having the harbour surveyed with this in mind as early as
1813.[4] The survey concluded that Fowey was 'better calculated than any
other harbour in the west of England for wet and dry docks on a scale
suitable for merchantmen'.[5] Treffry went ahead and built a quay and
ore-processing floors at Caffa Mill at the cost of £2000, accessing the
quay by a 250 foot shute from Hillhay to the riverside. He soon became

disillusioned, however, 'having found one hundred mules and nearly thirty wagon horses insufficient to bring the increased quantity of ores to Fowey'.[6] The hilly, five-mile route from his Fowey Consols mine, via Tywardreath to Hillhay, proved totally unsuitable for use by horse-drawn traffic carrying heavy loads, as this caused great damage to the roads. While Fowey vestry complained vociferously, and demanded Treffry use broad wheels on his wagons, Treffry himself demanded that the vestry should improve its roads. He also tried to solve the problem by building a railway direct from the mine to Fowey, with a tunnel under the Castle Dore to Golant road. In this he was thwarted by the objections of local landowners, notably William Rashleigh of Menabilly.[7]

Frustration at the shortcomings of the land links to Fowey led Treffry to take the decision to build a completely new port at Par between 1830 and 1837, despite the site being 'surveyed and condemned by some of the first engineers in the kingdom'.[8] A completely artificial harbour, it needed to be protected by the construction of a twelve-hundred-foot breakwater. Even then, Par was unable to service large ships. This split between the accessibility but poor situation of Par and the inaccessibility but excellent natural harbour of Fowey was to prove a lasting theme in the history of both ports. Treffry did, however, make land access to Fowey easier in the 1840s by improving the road from St Blazey and by excavating a new entrance, the New Road, at the top of the town. Plans for a bridge over the river, however, were never implemented.[9]

Despite the rapid expansion of the railway network after 1830, Cornwall remained unconnected to London until 1859, when the Great Western opened its line from Plymouth to Truro, following the completion of Brunel's Royal Albert Bridge over the Tamar.[10] The Lostwithiel and Fowey Railway was incorporated in 1862, but its completion was delayed by lack of funds and other problems until 1869. Designed to carry iron ore from a mine at Restormel, it was a broad gauge line on the west bank of the river, stopping at Upper Carne Point, half a mile above Fowey. Only five years later in 1874, however, the Cornwall Minerals Railway opened a rival freight line from St Blazey to Fowey, with jetties above Caffa Mill.[11] The company, given privileges over clay shipments, built hydraulic tipping frames for loading the clay at Fowey.[12] The Cornwall Minerals Railway, hoping to draw on growing tourist traffic, also opened a passenger service from St Blazey to Fowey in 1876, building a station at Fowey on land reclaimed from filling in part of Caffa Mill Pill.[13] The recognition that Fowey's port facilities needed to match the opportunity represented by the arrival of the railway was marked by an Act of Parliament in 1869. This established the Fowey Harbour Commission, charged with the development of the harbour.

The Lostwithiel and Fowey Railway struggled to compete with its rival, leading to its closure in 1880. Twelve years later, in 1892, its assets were sold to the Cornwall Minerals Railway, which extended its own line, now in standard gauge, to run from St Blazey to Lostwithiel. The two railways, previously separated not only by a gap between the ends of their respective lines but by different gauges, were now joined for the first time. The Cornwall Minerals Railway, in turn, was bought by the Great Western Railway in 1895.

It was these railways which built seven wooden jetties between Fowey and Upper Carne Point in the years between 1869 and 1895. China clay made up an ever-increasing percentage of what was loaded, rising from 61,000 tons in 1876 to over 600,000 tons in 1922.[14] When the Great Western was nationalised in 1948, its successor, British Rail, continued to own and run the docks at Fowey.

In the nineteenth century the china clay industry was split between up to seventy mostly small companies, with a joint capacity greater than the demand for its output. After the First World War, which badly disrupted production, three of the larger clay companies came together in April 1919 to form English China Clays, which established itself as one of Britain's leading companies.[15] Demand was sufficient to persuade the Great Western Railway to build a new jetty, as the existing ones were antiquated, causing long delays in the fulfilment of orders. A new No. 8 Jetty, costing £200,000, opened in 1923. At Upper Carne Point, it was the furthest of the eight jetties from the town.*

Production and shipment of china clay, sold to a wide range of customers in Europe and America, rose steadily in the 1920s. Following the Great Crash of 1929, however, a fall in output led to amalgamation

---

*   Only No. 4 Jetty had an electric elevator and conveyor belt. The other jetties simply had wooden chutes. Demand from America for china clay, which could only be met by shipping from a deep-water port, and the long delays at Fowey, led to English China Clays briefly supporting plans for an alternative outlet at St Just Pool. Other problems at Fowey included a shortage of rolling stock after the First World War. R. M. Barton, *A History of the China-Clay Industry* (Truro, 1966), pp. 167 and 170.

with two other sizeable china clay businesses, first with Lovering and then Pochin. Its full title became English Clays Lovering Pochin Company Limited.* During the Second World War, shipments again shrank, the quays being sealed off and used to ship explosives, stored for safety in quarries around Bugle. The harbour was also extremely active with naval traffic in the run up to D-Day in June 1944. After 1945, however, demand for china clay steadily increased, with a million tons shipped for the first time in 1955 from English China Clays' ports and two million tons reached in 1964.

This led to greatly increased activity at the port of Par, acquired on lease by English China Clays in 1946, before which it had been operated by its freeholder and original developer, the Treffry family. English China Clays only acquired the freehold in 1964. With the liquid clay arriving at Par in the company's network of underground pipes, much of the refining, drying and storage took place there. At its peak, Par had eleven driers and a number of stores, the largest of which could hold 40,000 tons. Par, however, had two major drawbacks. It was unsheltered and was not a deep-water port, the ships using it being restricted to 1500 tons, although this was later increased to 3000 tons. In the early 1960s Par was, nevertheless, the busiest port in the country per square foot of quay, with twelve berths constantly in use and another twelve ships often waiting to dock.[16]

The demand for china clay continued to grow and there seemed grounds for hope that three million tons would soon be shipped in a year. The bottleneck at Par, however, was a major constraint on English China Clays' plans. Although it would have been possible to improve the facilities at Par, this would have been both expensive and unsatisfactory. It would also have been at the expense of Fowey. It was realised that, if English China Clays proceeded with the project,

> it would make the port of Fowey obsolete, and rather than take this unilateral step of developing Par Harbour, they responded to an approach from British Rail ... to consider an alternative method of improving the port facilities used on developments at Fowey. Fowey has the natural advantage over Par of deep and weather protected

---

* For convenience, I have referred to it as English China Clays, ignoring its corporate components. By 1956 it had four divisions: china clay, building, quarrying and transport.

water suitable for 10,000 ton vessels, whereas Par would have to extend a considerable distance out to sea to attain the same depth of water.[17]

The overall cost of redeveloping Par, at £3,000,000, seemed also to be likely to be twice that of upgrading Fowey. The company's management therefore, encouraged by the approach from British Rail, decided to concentrate on Fowey. It commissioned a report from the consulting engineers Rendel, Palmer and Tritton in September 1966 as to the best way forward. Rendel, Palmer and Tritton submitted its report in July 1967, outlining three possible schemes but recommending one which contained most of the features of what was finally built.[*]

At the time, three of the jetties at Fowey were responsible for the bulk of the loading, handling 750,000 tons a year between them.[18] The aim of the development plan was to increase the tonnage shipped to 1,700,000 tons a year, with the scope to increase this further if necessary.[†] The scheme recommended dredging the river so as to allow ships of up to 15,000 tons to dock at No. 8 Jetty.[19] It also proposed a six hundred foot long quay, to replace Nos 5 and 6 Jetties, with storage space behind. 'The new quay would be sited on the shoal area of the river bend opposite Mixtow Pill so that vessels lying alongside it would not obstruct the main river channel.'[20] Nos 3 and 4 Jetties would continue to load clay brought by road. No. 8 Jetty would be extended by 180 feet (at the expense of Jetty 7, which would be demolished). Nos 1 and 2 Jetties, the nearest to Fowey, would not be used. The scheme was estimated at a cost of £2,121,000 and it was thought that it would take a little over two years to complete.

English China Clays came to an agreement with British Rail Western Region, formally signed in August 1968, by which it rented the docks for two hundred years. English China Clays would pay all the costs of modernising the docks, but British Rail would keep the right to ship other

---

* Rendel, Palmer and Tritton, 'Report on the Development of the Port of Fowey', July 1967. There is a copy in the archives of the China Clay History Society. The other schemes Rendel, Palmer and Tritton considered were simply extending and modernising No. 8 Jetty; or leaving No. 8 Jetty as it was but turning Jetties Nos 5 and 6 into a six hundred foot long quay.

† Most of what was shipped was bulk clay, making up 90 per cent of the total, with bagged clay (used to make plaster) making up the other 10 per cent. The quantity of imports through Fowey was and has remained insignificant.

clay producers' shipments via the port. British Rail would also sell English China Clays the line from Fowey to Par. It undertook to run a scheduled freight service from Lostwithiel to Fowey, bringing in clay from a number of pits, including ones in Devon. In return, English China Clays agreed to guarantee British Rail that it would ship at least 40 per cent of its exports by rail to Fowey. Alternatively, if it preferred to transport clay to Fowey by road, it would pay a toll on up to half a million tons of clay. Because of the narrowness of the site, there were no plans for processing at Fowey. Initially, the proposal was for four eighty-foot-high silos to be positioned behind Nos 5 and 6 Jetties.

Planning permission was sought for the development, under Section 9 of the Harbours Act (1964), on 28 November 1967. English China Clays took a positive line about the attraction of its new facilities:

> These proposals should retain Fowey as a viable commercial port without destroying the beauty and amenities of Fowey as a holiday and residential centre. The existing buildings and plant in the dock area could not be considered items of great attraction and the replacement of these antiquated items by modern designed port facilities should certainly add, rather than detract, from the appearance of the port.[21]

Once news of English China Clays plans became known, there was naturally disquiet in Fowey and, of course, Mixtow. According to the *Cornish Times*, 'While large-scale development of Fowey Docks would, undoubtedly, assist Fowey commercially, there are many fears in the town that its tourist trade, its main industry, will suffer'.[22] A particular fear was of greatly increased clay pollution. Two hundred local residents attended a public meeting at Fowey Town Hall on 18 September 1967, addressed by the local MP, Peter Bessell. The Town Council subsequently demanded a public inquiry, before backing down. Most criticism, however, was assuaged by English China Clays' assurance that the installation of 'the most modern handling equipment with special emphasis laid on the suppression of dust' would minimise clay pollution.[23] The solution of using the old railway track, through the Caffa Mill Valley, as a road seemed neatly to solve the problem of access and the threat of congestion.

Another threat was posed by a change in English China Clays' plans for storage at the new port facility. From four eighty foot silos, its plans changed to eight 120 foot silos. The threat of these eyesores was mitigated by a compromise between Mrs Anne Treffry of Place and the National Trust. According to a later National Trust leaflet:

> Essential to these plans was the construction of eight 120 foot high clay silos on the docks land. The need for such very tall silos only arose because of the confined area within which the ECC had to work.
>
> The land behind the docks, running from Station Wood through the old fields of Carne to Carne Wood at the southern end of Colvithick Wood, was owned by the Treffry family of Place. Mrs Anne Treffry, known locally as the Queen of Fowey, was well aware of the crucial role played by this land, and in 1966 gave it to the Trust in order to bring the Trust into the arena.
>
> Through negotiation and compromise with ECC, the Trust was able to allay Mrs Treffry's twin fears by solving an environmental crisis whilst not impeding Cornwall's major industry, which had a good export record and employed many local people. By leasing to ECC a small piece of the Treffry land, on the corner of Carne Wood, the Trust ensured that the clay storage shed subsequently built there was, whilst still large enough to be of use to ECC, much lower and less obtrusive than the eight silos first planned.[24]

English China Clays needed the approval of the Ministry of Transport for its main plan. Its Managing Director, Alan Dalton, had a meeting with the Minister, Barbara Castle, early in 1968.

> It was a great pleasure to meet you at the DEA on 31 January, and I was grateful for the opportunity it gave me to mention to you the subject of Fowey. The purpose of this letter is to enlist your active support to enable us to make up ground which we are losing as each day passes without a decision from your Ministry ... There is no doubt that on technical and financial grounds, and in the interests of exports from this country, this application is sound.[25]

Planning permission by the Ministry of Transport was given on 10 April 1968.

There were problems with the National Union of Railwaymen, over the future employment of its members, which were sorted out with some difficulty, with the men guaranteed jobs at the new docks. In contrast, there were amicable negotiations with the Fowey Harbour Commission and with the National Ports Council. Cornwall County Council, unwilling for a constant succession of trucks to block the roads between Fowey and Par, needed to be convinced about the viability of the proposed road link, via the Pinnock Tunnel, between Par and Fowey, which was to replace the railway line.*

Construction began in late 1968 and continued, in one form or another, for four years.[26] At the main construction site, Nos 5 and 6 Jetties, the quay was extended well into the river on a series of large piles.† Behind it, the rock was cut back and stabilised to allow space for the storage. Instead of silos, it was decided to build a single clay store, in the traditional shape of a linhay, with eight bays for different types of clay. Above the linhay, there are now more trees in Colvithick Wood than there were before the redevelopment.

Although levels of activity remained high in the 1970s, English China Clays suffered a severe downturn in the 1980s. The increasing use by paper-makers of calcium carbonate (made from chalk or marble, rather than clay) ate into English China Clay's 80 per cent share of the paper market. Calcium carbonate was half the price of clay. Although English China Clays' products retained an advantage in some forms of paper making, notably in coated as opposed to filled paper, its share of the market declined to 30 per cent.

A second blow to the industry's core business was the development of clay and carbonate sources outside Europe. Very high quality deposits of clay were discovered in the Amazon basin in Brazil. As secondary deposits, these beds were far easier to work than those in Cornwall.

------

* Also shown as the Pinnick Tunnel on early maps. Passenger trains had not run between Par and Fowey since 1934. The passenger service from Lostwithiel to Fowey was ended on 4 January 1965. On 28 November 1968, the *Cornish Times* reported a farewell to Fowey's passenger link to the outside world: 'On Tuesday last a social and film show were arranged by members of Fowey Parish Church, at which a nostalgic film, *Last Train to Lostwithiel*, was shown as well as other films of local interest. The filmed records of the last train were by Mr H. Smith and many sighs were to be heard as it ran its course. During the evening solos were sung by two members of the church choir – Miss Caroline Murray and Miss Claire Lugg – both of whom were accompanied on the piano by the parish church organist, Mr Norman Williams. A large crowd accompanied this very successful evening'.

† The space created allowed the establishment of a thriving mussel farm in the water beneath the deck of the quay.

Roughly speaking, ten tons of digging in Cornwall yielded one ton of clay, as against only four tons to produce the same quantity in Brazil.

Domestically, English China Clays also lost its way, being slow to wake up to the scale of the threats posed by these changes. Under a new chief executive, Andrew Teare, the company followed what proved to be an unsuccessful strategy between 1990 and 1995, selling parts of the company which would have been valuable in the long term, including its housing division and land holdings. Its concentration on its core china clay business was soon shown to have been misguided. In 1994, after its share price dropped by two-thirds, the company fell out of the FTSE index.

These disasters, which left the company vulnerable to outside forces, led to the sale of English China Clays to Imetal (later to become Imerys) in 1999. Despite heavy investment by Imerys in its new acquisition, in 2002 to 2004, Cornish clay continued to lose market share. Finally, Imerys decided to move its coated paper business to Brazil, where it had made major acquisitions. This led to 600 job losses in Cornwall in 2006 and 2007 and the closure of most of the facilities at Par, which may in future be developed as an environmentally sustainable housing estate under the title of Eco-Bos.[*]

Since then there has been more investment from Imerys. In November 2012 Imerys acquired Goonvean, which specialises in kaolin. Cornish clay still has a role to play in filled papers, ceramics and specialised building applications. The hope was that, with the contribution of Goonvean, the shipments of china clay and other freight through Fowey would stabilise at around 850,000 tons a year, with aggregate making up a part of the shipments. For the latest year for which figures are available, however, the total shipped was down to below 650,000. This shortfall may, however, be balanced in future by a substantial increase in aggregate shipping. If indeed the amount of shipped aggregate increases, this may lead to over a million tons being shipped again from Fowey annually.

---

[*]   The name was derived from *bos*, the word in the Cornish language for house. On 4 December 2012, however, Eco-Bos announced a scaling back of its ambitious plans for a flagship ecological town development. Four of the six staff working in its St Austell office were made redundant.

5

Modern Times

THE PATTERN OF change at Mixtow, some of it dating from before the war but becoming more clear-cut by the 1960s, reflected developments in Britain as a whole and Cornwall in particular. Communications between Cornwall and the rest of England improved, with the motorway reaching Exeter in 1977 (though sections of it were open well before this). People lived longer and Cornwall's population came to include a greater number of pensioners. Second homes became a commonplace ambition of the middle class and Cornwall's main industry changed from farming to tourism. The store set by families on an annual holiday, with increased leisure and the widespread ownership of cars, greatly increased the demand for holiday lets in Mixtow, Fowey and Cornwall as a whole. Yachting as a leisure and holiday interest also grew in popularity, with a steady growth in the numbers of small boats moored at Fowey. In Mixtow itself, the years after the war saw a number of new houses built and an increased population, though many of the houseowners no longer lived there full time; a trend which increased over the years which followed, as several of the houses, including the farmhouses, were converted partly or completely into holiday lets.

The first new house to be built at Mixtow after the war was Tonkins Quay House. This, immediately above Mixtow Quay on the river, was on the site of both an earlier limekiln, dating from the late eighteenth century, and of one of the numerous boathouses constructed by Edward

Atkinson in the 1890s. His cousin, Alice Rainey, had kept it for herself
when Mixtow House and Farm were sold to Robert Varco in 1915; and
Rosebank (soon to be Kits House) was sold to Frank Kilpatrick in 1919.
On her death in 1930, Alice Rainey had left the boathouse to her solicitor, Ernest Kite. He, in turn, sold it in 1937 to John Sutherland, a local
man who had had made a career as an electrical engineer in Malaya and
Sarawak. Among other things, Sutherland was a keen early radio enthusiast, being the first man to hold a Malayan broadcasting licence.

During the war, when Mixtow was taken over by the Navy, and used as
a landing-craft repair workshop by the Americans in 1944, the boathouse
had been damaged beyond repair. Soon after the war Sutherland and his
wife, Kathleen, built a new house to replace the boathouse, keeping the
latter's shape. They took up residence in 1947 and lived there until John
Sutherland's suicide on 17 June 1961.* The house was sold to Edith Smith
later in the same year. She in turn sold to Mary Farrant, who ran an
antiques shop in Lostwithiel; and then in 1971 to Victor Hoath, a retired
policeman, and his wife, Mary. Victor Hoath brought habits acquired in

---

*   A gun expert, who specialised in the intricate engraving of guns for leading
gunmakers, John Sutherland shot himself on the path on the north side of Mixtow
Pill. An obituary appeared in the *Journal of the Institution of Electrical Engineers*: 'John
George Alexander Sutherland who died in Cornwall on the 17 June 1961 was born on
14 November 1896. He was educated at Cornwall County School, Fowey, and received
his electrical engineering education from Mr H. Nimmo and his practical training
with the Great Western Railway Company at Fowey harbour works and power
station. In 1915 he joined Burroughs, Wellcome and Co., Dartford, in the electrical
engineering department. He served as a marine engineer during the 1914–18 war and
in 1919 joined United Engineers Ltd, Singapore, as an electrical engineer and gained
rapid promotion to manager of the electrical division. He also served as a director of
the Sarawak Electricity Supply Co., an associate company, and advised the Sarawak
Government on the installation of small power stations throughout that country. He
escaped from Singapore before the capitulation and returned to England, where he
served in the Ministry of Supply from 1942 to 1945. On the surrender of the Japanese
in 1945, he immediately returned to Singapore as acting managing director of United
Engineers and was responsible for the rehabilitation of that organisation until the
staff who had been interned returned from recuperation leave. He finally retired to
England in 1947, on account of ill-health, but continued as London director of United
Engineers until his death. He was an early radio enthusiast, a founder member of the
Malayan Amateur Broadcasting Society, and the first to own a Malayan broadcasting
licence. He is survived by his widow. He joined the Institution as an Associate
Member in 1929 and was elected a Member in 1937.'

the police force into retirement, patrolling Mixtow after the arrival of any new visitor.* Following his death in 1988, Mary Hoath kept Tonkins Quay House for five years before selling the house to Dave and Shirley Bieber. Dave Bieber, a British Airways pilot, continued John Sutherland's interest in radio by building an impressive communications mast facing Mixtow Quay. Capable of extension to a height of eighty feet, the mast only has planning permission for a height of sixty feet. The Biebers' yacht, *Crystal Eyes*, after some years in the Mediterranean but currently at Mixtow, is so called because it was acquired after Dave Bieber crystallised his British Airways pension to buy it.

When Robert Varco died, in January 1961, leaving £33,579 7s. 5d., Roger King, who had been renting No. 2 since 1936, was given first option of buying both No. 1 and No. 2. He bought both bungalows for £900 from Varco's estate, with the proviso that No. 1 should remain rented out to its current elderly tenants. These tenants were Mr and Mrs Arthur Greystones. Arthur Greystones was an old seadog who had sailed before the mast. He had also been in a gunboat on the Yangtse at the time of the Boxer Rebellion. His wife was a poor white, of Irish descent, from Jamaica. After the Greystones died, in the 1960s, Roger King kept No. 2 for himself but rented out No. 1 as a holiday let. In later life, Roger started going to Spain for holidays (one of many Britons who now went abroad, rather than to traditional seaside resorts at home), while his son Richard went out to work in Africa; but his other son, Simon, was often at Mixtow.[1]

One day a man arrived on a boat, introduced himself and said that he wanted to buy No. 1. This was George Miners, who had retired from the RAF Regiment as a flight lieutenant and was about to marry for the second time. His second wife, Rosemary, was an artist. Roger King was persuaded to sell No. 1, which was subsequently renamed Carpe Diem. An extra room at the top was put on as a painting studio for Rosemary. The Minerses lived there for ten years before Rosemary became ill. In the end, she had to be lifted out by helicopter. The couple subsequently moved to Lostwithiel and ended up in different old people's homes. She died first.

The second family, after the Kings, whose arrival marked the beginning of a long-term connection with Mixtow was that of the Browns.

---

* Irked by the predictability of his tread outside the windows of Mixtow House, to which I was then a new visitor, I counter-patrolled, to Victor Hoath's surprise, outside Tonkins Quay House. Hoath also grew Christmas trees to sell.

Leslie Clifford Brown, a solicitor, was the senior partner in Reed and Reed in King Square, Bridgwater.* He and his wife, Grace, had five children: Diana, Richard, Priscilla, John Julian and Naomi. With the exception of John Julian, who went to live in New Zealand, all the Brown children acquired an interest in Mixtow, either living there or using it as a holiday home.

Dick Brown had worked on a farm in Somerset and wanted to take up farming. After the war, Leslie Brown first rented, then bought Dorset Farm (previously farmed by John Girdlestone) for Dick to work. At this time it still had a Cornish stone farmhouse, on the north side of the farmyard. Leslie Brown employed an architect with the intention of restoring it, but it had been uninhabited for many years and was so dilapidated that a decision was made to pull it down. Instead, a galvanised house was built above the farmyard, where Vivian and Lorraine Sandy lived for some years.

In 1949, after the death of Archie Watty, Leslie Brown bought Watty's boathouse and the nearby cottage from Robert Varco. The house had acquired the name of Flagstaff Cottage, from a flagpole behind it at one time, and was originally given to his daughter Priscilla. After Leslie Brown's wife died, and Priscilla married Arthur Smart, the Browns used Watty's as a holiday home. Leslie Brown would sometimes come down by train for the day from Bridgwater to cut the lawn and to see that everything was in good order. The house and boathouse were later returned to Priscilla, who left it to her daughter, Penelope Tuck.[2]

After 1945 Mixtow Farm, with twenty-two acres, was rented by Mr and Mrs Marsh from Robert Varco. In 1949, after Mr Marsh died, Leslie Brown offered to buy the farm, but Varco did not want to sell it. So, instead, Brown rented it for twelve years, during which time Dick Brown lived there with his wife Pat, who had grown up in Polruan.† When Varco

---

*   Leslie Brown (1891–1981) went to school at the City of London School for Boys and was in the Indian Army in the First World War. He qualified as a solicitor: having failed at his first attempt, he came top in all England at his second in 1921. He and his wife, Grace Chaundler, were both born on 6 November 1891, within an hour of each other. They lived at Hamp House, Bridgwater. Grace's sister was Christine Chaundler, an author of several children's books. Information on the Brown family from Penny Tuck and Naomi Wilmot.

†   Dick Brown, who cut an unusual figure as a Cornish farmer, had attracted a good deal of interest from the girls of Polruan as a bachelor with a farm. Before he married, he had a housekeeper, Miss Stephen, who became the first secretary of the new village hall at Whitecross.

himself died, in 1961, his widow offered Leslie Brown the farm, which he bought. Brown then converted what had previously been a farmworker's cottage, a barn and a cider press into the present house, Mixtow Farm House, moving with his daughter Naomi from Bridgwater to live there after he retired from full-time work in 1969.* Dick Brown, in turn, moved to a bungalow above Dorset Farm, which had replaced the galvanised house, and lived there with Pat and their daughter, Lucil. Leslie Brown also bought additional land for Dick.

When Leslie Brown died, in 1981, Naomi inherited ten acres and Dick twelve acres of Mixtow Farm. Since Dick Brown's death in 1997, his daughter Lucil, who is married to another farmer, Arthur Jasper, and has two sons, Paul and Neil, has farmed Mixtow and Dorset Farms, although living at another farm, at Linkinhorne.

Another of Leslie Brown's daughters, Diana, who married Dick Allden, bought No. 1 from the Minerses. The Alldens gifted it to their son, Jonathan, and his wife Sally, the present owners.[3] Since 1981 Naomi Brown, who after her father's death married John Wilmot, has lived at Mixtow Farm. Paul and Penny Tuck, both university lecturers, spend the summer at Flagstaff Cottage, still better known as Watty's due to the fine boathouse immediately next to it, often with their son Alexander, a medical student.[4] An extension is currently being added to the cottage, which is also being modernised.

William Tapley, who had bought Kits House from Winifred Davies in March 1940, was born at Aish, a hamlet of Stoke Gabriel on the east bank of the River Dart between Totnes and Dartmouth in 1881.† According to the census of 1901, he was a student in the electrical works in Loughborough. By 1911 he was living at Washington House, Redbridge, Southampton, being described in the census of that year as an employer

---

* Leslie Brown continued to work part-time on legal matters. To enable him to communicate more easily with his office in Bridgwater, he (with the support of others at Mixtow) arranged with the Post Office for the installation of a post box in the lane outside Mixtow House. Even before it was converted, however, Mixtow farmhouse was large enough to allow its tenants before the war, Archie and Carrie Tippett, to take in paying guests.

† His father, also William, had been born in Liverpool but in 1891 was living in Devon on his own means, with his wife Jessie, William and two younger sisters. After the sale of the Mixtow Pill Estate, which he sold at the age of eighty-two, Tapley lived at The Shrubbery, Dawlish Road, Teignmouth.

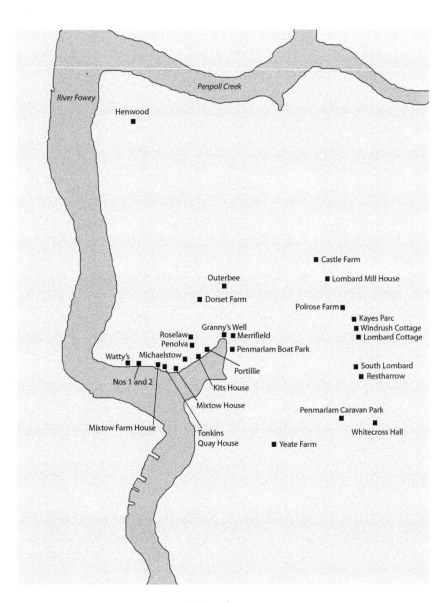

River Fowey

Penpoll Creek

Henwood ■

■ Castle Farm

Outerbee ■   ■ Lombard Mill House

■ Dorset Farm

Polrose Farm ■

Granny's Well   ■ Kayes Parc
Roselaw ■   ■   ■ Merrifield   ■ Windrush Cottage
Penolva ■   ■ Lombard Cottage
Watty's ■   Michaelstow ■ Penmarlam Boat Park
             ■   ■ South Lombard
Nos 1 and 2   ■ Portillie   ■ Restharrow

             Kits House

             Mixtow House

                                Penmarlam Caravan Park
                                      ■
Mixtow Farm House   ■
             Tonkins   Whitecross Hall
             Quay House   ■ Yeate Farm

Mixtow houses

and as a 'general engineer, repairs etc'. He had recently married and at this time he and his wife, Muriel, had a six-month-old son, William Paige Tapley.* Clearly a man of talent, Tapley took out no fewer than sixteen patents between 1921 and 1936. These ranged from an improved clamp to instruments for use in measuring acceleration and gradients. One of these inventions was a great success, being incorporated into a Stuart Turner engine. At Mixtow, he worked on his projects in the summerhouse of Kits House.

Over the years after the war, during which he was living at Kits House, Tapley accumulated other property nearby. He bought Mixtow House from Robert Varco in February 1946 for £1700. In addition, he bought back the site of Mixtow Bungalow, which had burned down in 1953, adjacent to Kits House. The site, which had been sold to Walter Olding of Lerryn for £100 in 1956, was bought by Tapley for £425 in 1960. This placed Tapley, now over eighty, in a position to put the two main houses in Mixtow, and the land around them, up for sale.

At 3 p.m. on 1 April 1963, a major day in the history of Mixtow, the Mixtow Pill Estate was auctioned at Fowey Town Hall, under the hammer of Nick Grose of May, Whetter and Grose.† The advertised estate comprised all the area requisitioned by the Navy during the war, with the exception of Tonkins Quay House. Tapley's property was described fulsomely in the auction brochure:

Mixtow Pill Estate is a quite exceptional property, offering seclusion and the enjoyment of the lovely Fowey Estuary. It is contained on the north side of a tidal creek, with about a thousand feet of water frontage and with a private quay and landing stage. The property enjoys a full southern aspect and there are magnificent views of the upper reaches of Fowey Harbour and over the creek.

The property has been in the same ownership for about seventeen

* William Tapley, who also owned four houses, numbers 14–17 Wellington Street, in Teignmouth, died only six months after the sale of the Mixtow Pill Estate, on 22 November 1963. Ill health may have contributed to his decision to sell the estate. He left £95,610 9s. 0d. The beneficiaries of his will were his sons Edward Tapley and William Paige Tapley. The latter, who drove around in a motor bike and sidecar, was also an engineer, but at one point ran an antiques shop in Lostwithiel. Will of William Tapley, dated 14 December 1952; proved 22 January 1964.

† Frank and Madge Norman were in the room. The auction was over very quickly.

years and it is now being offered in several lots as it is considered too large as a whole for the average owner occupier. Where possible, direct water frontage is offered with each lot and right of the use of the quay is included.

The seven lots were:

1.   Mixtow House
2.   Kits House
3.   Rosebank Cottage
4.   Freehold Building Site
5.   Freehold Building Site
6.   Meadow
7.   Garage/Boathouse

Although it was due to be offered in seven separate lots, in the event the estate was bought as a whole for £25,000 (The reserve price for the estate, under which the lots would have been sold off individually, was £20,000.)* The buyer was Frank Saxton, or rather his company, Globe Trailers Ltd.† For

---

*   Robert Saxton, while working in Ghana, remembers seeing the final price as £25,000 in a newspaper, a sum that is generally remembered as the correct one. It is unclear why his father paid more than the thousand pounds needed to top Hartley Pollard's bid of £21,000. Possibly other bidders pushed the price up. Unfortunately, May, Whetter and Grose have not kept their records from this period.

†   Frank Saxton (1900–1991) came from Birmingham, where his father had been a secondary school headmaster. His name was registered as Frank, but he was christened Harold, the name by which many people knew him. (He also had the trying middle name, given for family reasons, of Batty.) He went to Birmingham University, but did not finish his course. A member there of the Officer Training Corps, he avoided call-up only because the First World War ended three weeks after his eighteenth birthday. Due to a motor cycle accident in 1926, which left him in hospital for eighteen months, he had a limp and walked with a stick. He was otherwise physically strong, living to be almost ninety-one. Saxton took up teaching and was the headmaster of a village primary school at Shenstone in Staffordshire between 1934, when he married, and 1946. Although good at it, and well respected, he had no wish to spend his whole life as a teacher. He met his wife, Freda, through teaching. She came from an artistic family in the Potteries, where her father, Ernest Light, was the head of Hanley Art School. A sculptor and ceramic designer, Light created a number of Doulton figurines and Wedgwood black basalt designs. The family were strict Methodists, while Frank Saxton enjoyed driving powerful cars, which had the advantage of being easier to drive with his bad leg and were better for towing

holidays after the war, Frank Saxton and his wife, Freda, had had a caravan at Brean Down, near Weston-super-Mare. Having acquired an interest in caravans, Saxton had the idea of building and selling them, buying a small Birmingham company, Globe Trailers Ltd. The company employed twenty or thirty people and produced a number of caravans. He subsequently built up a business dealing in second-hand caravans in Birmingham. Pursuing caravans from another angle, Saxton bought Yew Tree Farm in 1954, centred on a fine farmhouse, at Berrow, near Burnham on Sea, and got permission to turn the land around it into a caravan site. He sold the house and caravan site in 1957. He subsequently bought a number of large houses, including ones at Arnewood in the New Forest and two in Northam, near Bideford, in north Devon.* He combined living in the houses with selling off the land around them at a profit. In 1963 he had recently sold Marchwood, the second house at Bideford, and came to the Mixtow Pill Estate armed with the proceeds of this sale and a short-term loan from Lloyds Bank.

Having bought the estate as a whole in the auction room, Frank Saxton immediately sold on parts of it to the underbidders, though he kept Kits House (Lot 2) and the meadow (Lot 6) for himself. It was said that he got his money back by the time he left the auction room. What is certainly true is that he speedily sold off five of the other lots to the underbidders or interested parties:

1.	Mixtow House	John Carlyon	£8000
3.	Rosebank	Kenneth Pearce	£4500
4.	Portillie	Hartley Pollard	£2500
5.	Michaelstow	Charles Boldero	£1500
7.	Granny's Well	Goronwy Jones	£1000
	Total		£17,500

---

caravans. He also enjoyed going to the pub. He was, however, a social rather than a heavy drinker and was a safe driver. I am most grateful to Frank and Freda Saxton's daughter, Hilary and their son, Robert, for information about their father and about the Mixtow Pill Estate.

* Saxton was already familiar with the area from an earlier caravan holiday at Killgarth Manor, Polperro. According to Robert Saxton, his father first saw about the sale of the Mixtow Pill Estate in a newspaper used to wrap some fish and chips he had bought. He may also have had an adviser in north Devon who tipped him off about the estate.

A year later, on 9 September 1964, he also sold the land immediately above Kits House to Joseph Waller for £3200, leaving Kits House itself with only a small garden. This brought Saxton's income from the post-auction sales to £20,700, meaning that he had paid £4300, amply covered by the proceeds of his sale in Bideford, for Kits House and the meadow.* The conveyances to the underbidders, all finalised by the autumn of 1963, formed part and parcel of the conveyance of the Mixtow Pill Estate to Frank Saxton, with William Tapley endorsing the sale of the constituent pieces.

John Carlyon, a regional director of Barclays Bank, whose address at the time of the auction was The Old Rectory, Doynton, Gloucestershire, bought Mixtow House for £8000 and lived there for four years. A car accident at Grampound, however, meant that he had to wear a neck brace and couldn't turn his neck, which made living at Mixtow impracticable. Mixtow House was bought from Carlyon for £12,000 in 1967 by Charles and Stella Poole, whose family still owns the house.† Charles Poole, known generally as Bill, had strong local connections in Fowey. He was a grandson of Sir Charles Augustin Hanson, who built Fowey Hall.‡ Born in Fowey, and in his early life a Wesleyan preacher, Hanson went out

---

*   These figures, and other details about the sale, are taken from the conveyances from Globe Trailers Ltd to the buyers, with the exception of Rosebank, which comes from Kenneth Pearce's daughter, Lyn Carter. I have given the names of the houses existing or later built on the respective plots. The plot sold to Joseph Waller was later used for the sites of Yarkhill (now Penolva) and Roselaw. I am very grateful to Dave and Shirley Bieber, George Seppings and Penny Tuck for allowing me to see the title-deeds to their houses.

†   It is possible, in making his decision to sell Mixtow House, that John Carlyon was aware that the imminent redevelopment of the docks opposite might reduce the house's attraction.

‡   Sir Charles Augustin Hanson (1846–1922), the son of Joseph and Mary Hanson, was born in Fowey. (His father, a master mariner, was swept overboard in the Bay of Biscay while his children were still young.) He emigrated to Canada as a Wesleyan minister. Discovering he had a great aptitude for finance, he set up a successful company, Hanson Brothers, in Canada before returning to England in 1890 and becoming Chairman of the Gresham Life Assurance Society. He was a JP for Cornwall and for the county of London; High Sheriff of Cornwall and Sheriff of London; Alderman of the City of London, 1909–21; Lord Mayor of London, 1917–18; and Deputy Lieutenant for Cornwall. He was created a baronet in 1918. A Unionist, he was elected unopposed for the Bodmin Division of Cornwall in August 1916, when the sitting member stood down, and sat until his death on 17 January 1922.

to Canada and made a fortune. Coming back, he became Lord Mayor of London in 1917–18 and MP for Bodmin.

Bill Poole's father, General Sir Frederick Poole, had married Alice Hanson in St Fimbarrus, Fowey, in 1906.* Living at Cotswold House in Fowey, they had two sons, Bill in 1907 and Robert in 1909. Frederick Poole had retired from the army as a major in February 1914 to avoid the risk to his young family of a posting to Jamaica. Recalled to the army on the outbreak of war in August 1914, he rose rapidly in rank as an artillery commander on the Western Front. Sent to Russia in December 1916, he commanded the British landing at Archangel in July 1918. Retiring from the Army in 1920, he lived at Torfrey in Golant until his death in 1936. Lady Poole died in 1952.

Bill Poole had an early interest in radio and opened a number of radio shops, including one in Fowey, the Fowey Radio Company, which continues today as Bartletts. After the war, in which he served in the Royal Corps of Signals in the Middle East, he became a solicitor and practised in St Austell. Stella Poole, in contrast, came from an academic family in Cambridge. With their children, Geoffrey, Henry and Lucy, the Pooles had previously lived in Lostwithiel. Bill Poole lived at Mixtow until his death in 1976, while Stella Poole lived there until her own death in 2009. After her husband's death, she converted part of Mixtow House into a separate cottage as a holiday let.

After buying the Mixtow Pill Estate, Frank Saxton lived initially at Kits House, before moving into Edward Atkinson's art gallery and making it into a separate house, called Kits Cottage. He did this by putting a ceiling into the part of the gallery nearest to Kits House, to make room for several bedrooms. He then turned the main part of Kits House into four letting flats. The Saxtons moved from Mixtow to retire to the Isle of Man in 1970, partly as a result of Frank Saxton's distrust of what might happen after the election of Harold Wilson's Labour government. He sold

He married Martha Sabina Applebe, the daughter of James Applebe, Esq., of Halton, Canada, in 1868.

* Frederick Poole had met Alice Hanson in 1906, whilst on sick leave from service in Nigeria, when staying at Penarwyn, in St Blazey. Penarwyn was the home of his sister, Mary, who had married John Treffry. All shared an interest in hunting. John Treffry was the master of the Fowey Harriers from 1883 to 1897 and from 1900 to 1925. Information from Henry Poole.

Kits House to Reg and Elizabeth Tomlin; and Kits Cottage to Jack and
Menny Turner.

Frank Saxton died on the Isle of Man at the age of ninety in 1991. It is
unclear how successful his business was, though it enabled him to live in
some style in large houses in pleasant areas of the country. Apt to drive
a hard bargain, and well aware of the value of money, Saxton's business
instincts were offset by the kindness of his wife. He never went ahead
with a business deal without getting her approval. Freda died at Sidmouth
in 2002, aged ninety-one, having remarried happily at the age of eighty-
six. After Frank Saxton's death his son, Robert, scattered his ashes on the
beach at Mixtow.* He later also scattered his mother's ashes there.

Rosebank Cottage, Lot 3 in the sale, which had until then been part of
Kits House, was sold off by Frank Saxton immediately after the Mixtow
Pill Estate auction to Kenneth and Mary Pearce for £4500. (Rosebank
retained the name of its larger neighbour, when this changed its name to
Kits House between the wars.) Kenneth Pearce owned a leather-finishing
firm in Northampton, which was in a fine Art Deco building. The house,
which has been kept by the Pearce family since 1963, and is now owned
by Kenneth and Mary Pearce's children, has mainly been used as a letting
property.[†]

Lot 4, the larger building plot of half an acre, was sold on for £2500
by Saxton immediately after the auction to Hartley Pollard, a chartered
accountant from Mevagissey.[‡] (Pollard had been an underbidder for the

---

* Frank Saxton was domineering, according to his daughter, Hilary; or stern
but fair, according to his son, Robert. He was a practical man who was very good with
his hands, especially at carpentry. He often put in the kitchens into the houses he
was converting himself. He kept good business records. Prevented by his leg from
sailing, he enjoyed going out in his motor boat.

† The current owners are Lyn Carter, Sally Dark, David Pearce and Jonathan
Pearce. Chris Dark, Sally's husband, at one point ran a bookshop in Lostwithiel.
Kenneth Pearce also wrote a history of Mixtow, but I have not yet seen a copy.
Information from Lyn Carter.

‡ Hartley Pollard's father and elder brother both spent their lives at sea, in the
merchant navy and as a fisherman respectively. Although Hartley himself made a
career as an accountant, including working as company secretary for Trelawney Ltd
at Marazion and Goodbody's in Plymouth, in retirement he wanted to live somewhere with good access to the sea. For this, the Fowey estuary was ideal. His wife,
Anne, a keen gardener who laid out the garden at Portillie, came from London. Of
his two sons, Christopher was tragically killed in an airline accident in Stockport in
1967. Ginny Pollard was born in Plymouth but grew up in Uganda, though her family

whole Mixtow Pill Estate, offering £21,000 for it. He had been unable to attend the auction himself, being represented there by his wife and brother-in-law.) Hartley Pollard built a house on his plot, finished in 1966 and named Portillie, the English name for Mevagissey. It is unusual in that, although designed by Pollard, it came in sections from builders in Kent called Colt. Its walls are of reformite, an artificial stone made, after the extraction of china clay, from the quartz residue. Most of the wood is cedar (with the beneficial result that there are no moths), but there is also some pine.* Hartley and Anne Pollard lived in Portillie until their deaths. Since then it has been owned by John and Ginny Pollard. Between 1970 and 2008, they lived in Northern Ireland, where John Pollard was a Lecturer in Geography, at the University of Ulster in Coleraine, and Ginny taught in a primary school. After Anne Pollard's death in 1986, Portillie was used for holiday lets until John and Ginny returned to live there full time.

The smaller building lot, Lot 5 of a quarter of an acre, was bought by Charles Boldero for £1500. Boldero, of Woodside, Puriton Hill, Bridgwater, worked for British Cellophane at Bridgwater and almost certainly knew Leslie Brown. He built a bungalow called Michaelstow on the lot and lived there for a while before selling it to Jack Turner, after Turner and his wife, Menny (who had previously been living at Kits Cottage), separated. Rodney and Nancy Hall, who were local farmers, owned it after Jack Turner's death. It was then bought by Jason Thompson and his wife, Christine, a librarian. Jason, a management consultant, was badly treated by Johnson's, the giant pharmaceutical company based in Kalamazoo, Michigan, famous for its baby powder, for whom he did a major reconstruction exercise. The present owners are Paul and Janet Harvey.† The Harveys decided to live at Michaelstow, which they bought in 2006, when Paul retired.

Lot 6, a meadow of one and three-quarter acres, was kept by Frank

---

left Uganda after it became independent. John and Ginny Pollard have four children, Rebecca, Philip, Edward and Rachel. Information from John Pollard.

    *   If the house is ever demolished, Colt has expressed a willingness to buy back the valuable cedar.

    †   Paul Harvey is a retired builder from Ealing. Janet Harvey's father, George Huckle, was an architect who designed the three houses, built in the 1960s, in Barr's Close above Bodinnick. The landowner had one, one was sold to pay for the development, but Huckle kept one. Information from Paul and Janet Harvey.

Saxton until he left Mixtow. He then sold it to his daughter Hilary and her husband, Roy Severn, who later became Professor of Civil Engineering at Bristol University and was a leading expert on arch dams and on the prevention of earthquake damage. Severn provided the money for the purchase. Roy and Hilary, and their two daughters, Fiona and Elizabeth, spent many holidays at Mixtow, living either in a tent or in a caravan. The Severns tried to get planning permission to turn what had been a cowshed into a house, but this was refused.

The final lot, Lot 7, yet another of Edward Atkinson's boathouses at the head of Mixtow Pill, sometimes used as a garage, was bought by Goronwy Jones, of Welsh Street, Chepstow, Monmouth, for £1000. He sold it on to Major John Lewis, who had recently retired from the Blues and Royals and was living in Fowey. Lewis and his wife, Honor, bought it with the intention of building a house on it. The Lewises got planning permission to convert the boathouse into a garage (below) with a bungalow from a standard design book (above).

Visitors to Cornwall who were looking for somewhere to build a house talked by chance to a local man called Williams, who was using fifty-gallon oil-drums to float away pig-iron from the wreck of the *Mauvereen* at Mixtow. This led to a meeting with 'The Major'. The Lewises had by this time decided against living at Mixtow, as Honor Lewis preferred to be near the Royal Fowey Yacht Club. The Lewises therefore sold on the plot, with planning permission, to these visitors, who were Bill and Kath Peacock.[*]

Bill Peacock was the co-owner of an engineering business at Alperton, while living in Hartington Road in Chiswick. The Peacocks, and Bill's business, subsequently moved to Andover, responding to a grant available under the Expanded Towns Policy. (Their house in Hartington Road became the London home of their daughter and son-in-law, Maggie and Richard Davies, both architects.) As part of the business, Bill Peacock

---

[*]   Before buying the plot for Granny's Well, Bill and Kath Peacock, assisted by Maggie and Richard Davies, their daughter and son-in-law, had over a period of nine months conducted an extensive search along the south coast for somewhere to live in their retirement. The Davieses had already stayed at one of the National Trust cottages at Pont. On a second visit to the cottage, Bill and Kath came with them. They looked at a variety of properties near Fowey, including what subsequently became the recording studios at Woodgate Pill. Information on the Peacocks and Granny's Well from Richard and Maggie Davies.

ran a motor car racing team, which included winning Formula Ford and Formula V teams (the latter based on Volkswagen components). His father had been involved in the earliest days of cars, working for the Electric Cab Company in 1889. Bill was also an expert on early cars, hunting out and restoring (amongst others) a 1903 Argyll, a 1904 Darracq, a 1910 Humber Taxi and a 1921 Mercedes. Some of these cars, which he managed to buy very cheaply, he found decaying in a field in Odiham, near Basingstoke. Another rich haul, of twelve vintage cars and a First World War Red Cross ambulance, emerged from beneath rubble in Leyton. In a bombed out house in Wimbledon Bill discovered three early Mercedes, including one with silk upholstery. His main passion, however, was for the Gwynne 8 cars made in Hammersmith in the 1920s.

After considering retirement for some time, Bill Peacock finally sold his share of the business to his partner, who made him a good offer which included a life pension as part of the benefits. Having bought the boat-house from the Lewises, the plans were redesigned by Maggie and Richard Davies to replicate Bill and Kath Peacock's house in Andover, with a work-shop and boathouse below for Bill, and a garden surrounding the house for Kath. The Davieses suggested the addition of a loft, reached by ladder, to allow them, and Bill and Kath's grandchildren, James, Giles and Ben, to stay in the house. The house worked well, with Bill indulging his passion for vintage cars and boats, and mending anything requiring mending for his neighbours. A keen sailor, Bill had a Morecambe Bay prawner called *Radium*, dating from 1904. Bill, Jack Turner and Den Banham also spent many happy hours doing up *Fu Hsing*, a Chinese junk, and occasionally sailing in her. Kath, who was very good with people, became a popular local figure. She and Bill also specialised in making potent home-made brews, including a batch of carrot whisky especially popular with their friend, Jack Turner. The house had a liability, as it came with a clause entitling the Lewises to keep a boat in the garage of Granny's Well for the payment of a peppercorn rent.*

---

* Richard and Maggie Davies are distinguished architects, whose business MRDA, based in London, has overseen the restoration and upkeep of major and minor buildings in Cornwall. These include Truro Cathedral and St Michael's Mount, as well as St Fimbarrus in Fowey and St Ildierna in Lansallos. They have also been responsible for a number of conversions at Mixtow itself, including turning part of Mixtow House into a letting cottage for Stella Poole. They have recently completed a major extension at Granny's Well, doubling its size.

KITS HOUSE HOTEL

Between the wars, Rosebank had been renamed Kits House, to recall the name given to it in Sir Arthur Quiller-Couch's novels about Fowey, in which it was the house of Mr Fogo. Its old name of Rosebank was kept only by the cottage which had once been called Rose Hill. Frank Saxton sold Kits House, which he had converted into four letting flats, to Reg and Elizabeth Tomlin (the latter from Polruan), who turned it into a hotel. They did it up very much in the style of the seventies, with plastic wall tiles and other garish fittings. The Tomlins, who suffered a personal tragedy when their daughter, Caroline, died young, sold the hotel to Colin and Sheila Cheadle, retired local doctors. The Cheadles refitted the hotel in better taste. Under their ownership the hotel had nine bedrooms, seven of which had 'a beautiful view down the river to the small towns of Fowey and Polruan'. As well as arranging 'all manner of waterborne outings', Kits House Hotel specialised 'in the best English cooking' and aimed 'to provide a casual house party atmosphere with the comfort of a private home and the facilities and service of a hotel'.[5] Sheila was an excellent hostess and Colin, assisted at times by Dave Baker, ran a convivial bar. After two years, however, the Cheadles sold on the hotel in turn to Jeremy and Cleo Saise.

The hotel never proved easily profitable. It was not large enough to be run by staff, but it was too large to be run by its owners alone. Jeremy Saise was also unfortunate enough to lose an arm, when his car turned over near Dorset Farm. The Saises decided to convert it back into letting properties, adding two apartments, Bosun's Loft and Captain's Loft, reached from the back of the house. They finally sold Kits House, with its two lofts, to Richard and Christina Geering in 2005. Richard Geering, a retired vet with a special interest in horses, as a career taught animal science and basic physiology to medical and veterinary students at Imperial College. He and Christina bought Kits House as somewhere interesting to live, but which could be let out. They spend their winters in the Pyrenees. Kits House, despite the numerous changes through which it has gone, retains a number of distinctive features from the days of Edward Atkinson. These include several fine doorways and fireplaces.

Frank Saxton had sold the original Kits Cottage to Jack Turner in 1970, who lived there with his wife Menny. Turner was a retired businessman who had spent much of his early career working in South America. After the war, he was the managing director of a textile company in the north of England. Besides putting an extension onto the house, the Turners added a swimming pool, where there was previously a lawn. This was later filled in, following an accident. A fine Victorian conservatory, built by Atkinson, survived to coexist with the pool but has since been demolished.

Menny Turner joined the Southcottians, a sect founded by Joanna Southcott, a farmer's daughter from Devon. Southcott announced in 1813, at the age of sixty-four, that she was going to give birth to the new Messiah. The sect, which survived the non-fulfilment of this prophecy, believes that the Second Coming will be in Bedford, to which Menny Turner moved. This led to the Turners' divorce.* Subsequently, Kits Cottage was bought by Alan Tonkin, an Australian of Cornish descent, and his wife, Helen, who passed it on to David Blackburn, the ex-husband of their daughter. It was then bought by Nick Cowan, who owned and rented out student accommodation in Sheffield. When he was advised by his accountant to relocate to Guernsey, Cowan sold it to Richard and Christina Geering. This enabled the Geerings to reunite Kits House and Kits Cottage. As Kits Cottage had a separate approach, from the lane between Portillie and Roselaw, they renamed it Creekside to avoid confusion.

The meadow (Lot 6 in the Mixtow Pill Auction) was jointly cleared by the Peacocks, Davieses and Severns. On the advice of Bristol University's

---

* Menny Turner had been christened Menin, after the Menin Gate in Ypres. She once left a Southcottian tract on Stella Poole's pillow, when the latter stayed at Kits Cottage following the death of her husband, and said to her, 'Stella, I think I have been sent to you'. Stella replied, 'It's all right, Menny, you see I'm C of E'. After his divorce from Menny, Jack Turner, who died in 1997 and is buried at Lanteglos, moved to Michaelstow, the bungalow immediately above Mixtow House.

agricultural research facility at Long Ashton, it was planted with 250 jointly-owned French and Cornish apples. (Long Ashton was working on a project to persuade farmers to stop making cider containing wood alcohol, which sent many of them blind at fifty and killed them at fifty-five.) The apples were pressed at Penpoll and, though not ideally suited to the winder press there, produced excellent cider. After their daughters grew up, the Severns rarely visited Mixtow. The caravan, left abandoned, had to be dismantled and removed. In the end, the Severns sold the orchard, including the cowshed, to Richard and Maggie Davies, who inherited Granny's Well from the Peacocks after Bill's death in 2004.

Two other houses were built above the pill on the plot taken by Frank Saxton in 1963 from the land belonging to Kits House. Joseph Waller, of Tree Tops, Wraxall, Somerset, a bank manager, had bought the plot, bordering the lane between Mixtow House and Dorset Farm, for £3200. Here he and his wife, Norma, built a substantial house on two levels with a fine view over Fowey Harbour. The house was called Yarkhill, after a village in Herefordshire. Subsequent owners were Colonel Frank Stretch and his wife Margaret. Stretch, who had retired from the army, worked for Price Waterhouse. He later became part of a consortium which bought the Fowey Hotel. His wife Margaret didn't enjoy living and Mixtow, as she preferred Fowey. The Stretches sold the house to Sheila and Colin Cheadle, who continued to live there when they were running Kits House as a hotel. The Cheadles, in turn, sold Yarkhill to Ron and Linden Blake. Ron Blake worked as an engineer for the South West Electricity Board and Linden was a maths teacher. In 2009, when Linden Blake, now a widow, moved to Lostwithiel, it was bought by Dr Helen Doe, a maritime historian, and her husband, Mike Carter, who renamed it Penolva.

As Yarkhill only took half of the available plot, a second house was built next door, called Roselaw and completed in 1981. Initial plans to build the house seem to have met with difficulties over planning and finance. A company run by Kneale Layton, to whom Margaret Stretch sold the plot for development, went into liquidation. It was the liquidators of his company, Maycrain Ltd, who sold the house to Dr and Mrs Peter Rawlins, who built Roselaw. Peter Rawlins was a Harley Street doctor who once had the temerity to tell Stella Poole that she was obese. When the Rawlinses decided to move to Polruan, they sold Roselaw to Philip and Kathleen Selbourne. The Selbournes' cat, Melody, moved to live with the Peacocks, who renamed it Umbrage. The house's current owner is George

Seppings, from Enfield, who used to run a successful classic car restoration company near Potters Bar.

Although there was an earlier house on the site of Merrifield, at the head of Mixtow Pill, last mentioned in the census of 1841, the current house dates back only to the 1950s. It seems to have been built by Walter Olding, who had had a career as a tea planter. He had previously bought and sold the site of the burnt-out Mixtow Bungalow.[6] Initially built illegally, the new Merrifield subsequently got retrospective planning permission. Since then, it has changed hands several times. One house originally, Merrifield has also been expanded. The first owner, Mrs Teale, a teacher from Lanreath, kept donkeys. The second was a publican from Fowey, who developed cancer. The third couple were the Hamleys, who had a gift shop in Bude and subsequently one in Looe. Richard Davies designed an extension to Merrifield for them, but Mr Hamley built it himself completely differently, without reference to the approved plans. The Hamleys subsequently moved to Torquay, to open yet another gift shop. The fourth owners were Peter and Ginette Ayres. Peter Ayres was a retired builder, who had worked in Berkshire and Wiltshire, while Ginette was a teacher. They had earlier in Peter's career lived in Saudi Arabia, in Khobar after which the couple named their yacht. They subsequently moved to New Zealand, to be near their two children, who had emigrated, but Peter sadly died after only two years there. The piece of road above the ramp leading down to the water has been the subject of endless disagreement. Due to the build-up of nearby walls, there is now little space for boats and no space for parking at what is a council slipway open to the public.

Frank and Sue Ashworth, who previously lived in Blackheath, bought Merrifield in 2008. Frank is a lecturer in ceramics, while Sue is a stain-glass designer. They are the main makers of blue plaques to mark where famous people have lived in London. In all, they have made two hundred plaques, though some of these were privately commissioned. Although they look modestly sized, when affixed to walls in London, blue plaques are in fact substantial in size, being 19.5 inches across and weighing 16 kilos each. Hand-made and lettered by tube-lining, the plaques are fired in a kiln at Merrifield.*

Having been aware of Mixtow for some years, the Ashworths looked

---

* Frank and Sue Ashworth discovered Mixtow when they came on holiday to Fowey in 1996. They have a friend, Graham Jones, a well-known glass-designer, who lives in Lerryn. When they first arrived in Mixtow, in an inflatable with a motor and sails, they met a hospitable welcome from a relation of the then owners of Merrifield,

seriously for somewhere to buy near Fowey in 2007. After trawling through all the estate agents in Fowey, they decided against Fowey itself, as being steep and crowded, with the sun disappearing by 2 p.m. When they found Merrifield was for sale, they sold their Blackheath house, which had a fifty feet long conservatory, and moved to Mixtow.

Two of the main traditional farmhouses, those of Lombard and Yeate, are no longer connected with farming, while Dorset Farm's farmhouse was pulled down in the 1960s. Only Castle Farm is still run from its own farmhouse. During the war, Mary Libby and her son, Sydney, had farmed Castle Farm. The farm was subsequently bought by William Turpie of Highgate Farm in St Veep. Turpie's daughter, Madge, had met and married Frank Norman in 1957, while she was working in Cumberland. They lived together for three years at Oughterby, Kirkbampton, near Carlisle, before moving to Bodinnick in 1960, intending to look for a farm in Devon. In the end, they bought Castle Farm from Madge's father and ran it as a mixed dairy farm until 1991. Following an accident to Frank, they passed on the farm to their son, Iain. Iain and his wife, Beverley, who works as a podiatrist, now live in the farmhouse. Castle Farm, with ninety acres, has bullocks and around forty dairy cows; it is the only farm in Mixtow still to produce milk.

On the lane down to Mixtow, on Castle Farm's land, is Outerbee, a bungalow built by Frank Norman, who constructed it himself, with the exception of tiling the roof. Intended originally to be a house for a farm worker, its position was suggested by the local council to avoid it showing over the skyline, as it would have done nearer to Castle Farm itself. Its construction took a long time, between 1972 and 1991. When their son, Iain, married in 1991, Frank and Madge Norman moved to Outerbee, allowing their son Iain and Beverley Norman to move to Castle Farm itself. They named their bungalow after Oughterby, where Frank and Madge had once lived in Cumberland, but simplified the spelling of its first syllable and varied that of its third syllable, to reflect Frank's keeping of bees.[7]

The other working farm, Dorset Farm, continues to be purely a farming concern. It is now farmed by Lucil Jasper and her family, though there is

---

who was helpful about the possibility of launching the inflatable from the end of Mixtow Pill. Information from Frank and Sue Ashworth.

no longer a house there, other than the unoccupied bungalow above it. There are between twenty and twenty-five suckler cows on the farm.[8]

In the years after the war Lombard Farm was farmed by John and Percy Ferris, the sons of Colin Ferris. John Ferris, and his wife, Olga, and their five children, lived at Lombard Farmhouse, while Percy lived at Pont near his mother.* Later, Percy Ferris moved to Highway and finally to a new bungalow he built, Kayes Parc, just above Lombard farmhouse. The brothers, who ran Lombard as a mixed farm, bought the freehold of the farm from the Boconnoc Estate in the early 1970s. They then sold it to Arthur Miller, by which time its farmhouse was in a poor condition. When Miller himself died, in 1996, his widow decided to sell the farm at auction in three lots:

1.   The farmhouse and the field in front of it
2.   Two barns
3.   The 300 acres of farmland

In the event, two days before the auction, Lots 1 and 2 were bought by Dave and Catherine Collins. The arable land in Lot 3 was bought by a local landowner, Jeremy Goodenough, while the permanent pasture and woodland bordering the river was bought by the National Trust.

At the time he and his wife Catherine bought Lombard Farmhouse, Dave Collins was a project manager living in Southampton, involved in the sail-training ship *Tenacious*. After the Collinses moved to Lombard Farm, they did up the farmhouse and turned the nearby outbuildings, which were in very poor condition, into holiday lets. Dave Collins was for a time deputy harbour master in Fowey. He then became very actively involved for six years in Adventure Cornwall, based at Churchtown Farm, opposite Lanteglos church. Extending their holiday letting, the Collinses now have a yurt, a tepee and a cabin for glampers in the only field still belonging to Lombard Farm.[9]

Lombard Farm's stone barns, with a roundhouse, bordering the lane across from Lombard Farmhouse (not the ones sold in 1996), and much

---

* Colin and Mabel Ferris had four sons. Besides Jack and Percy, there were Charles, who farmed at Trevarder, and Brian, who became a teacher. Jack Ferris married Olga Norman in 1946, but she was not related to Frank Norman's family. Percy married in 1960 and had two daughters, Anne and Jane., but his wife, Peggy, died young.

of Lombard Farm's land had already been sold by Arthur Miller to Chris White. The barns have now been turned into a sizeable modern house, Lombard Mill House, for White and his wife, Dawn. White, originally a local builder, recognised early on the opportunity presented by the need to dig fibre-optic cables. Having specialised in this initially in Cornwall, he now has a highly successful business digging fibre-optic cables in Dubai and other Middle Eastern countries.

During the war, the lease of Yeate Farm was held by Richard Carnall. Following Carnall, who is remembered as having walked with a limp, the lease passed to Francis Devonshire and then to David Oliver. David Oliver, and his wife Angela, bought the freehold of the farm from the Boconnoc Estate in 1991. While he did some farming himself, Oliver, whose main personal interest was fishing, rented out most of Yeate Farm's land to Norman Rounsevell of Hall Farm. David Oliver later sold nearly all of Yeate Farm's farmland to Roy Burrows, keeping only the farmhouse and its outbuildings himself. These were then turned into holiday lets and are now owned by David and Angela Oliver's children, Rachel and Nick. Oliver also began a caravan park, Penmarlam, which he sold off to the Fowey Harbour Commission in 2001. In addition, he sold off the freeholds of Windrush Cottage and Restharrow, both of which had originally been labourer's cottages.

Roy Burrows, a hydraulics engineer rather than a farmer, continued to rent out Yeate Farm's agricultural land to Norman Rounsevell. Burrows put in, however, for planning permission on a couple of plots he retained between Restharrow and Lombard farmhouse. On one of these, he built a farm bungalow. The bungalow was, however, left uninhabited for a number of years and got into poor condition. Then in 1996 Peter Norman, Frank and Madge Norman's elder son, who had previously been living at Pen y Bryn at Highway, bought Yeate's farmland off Burrows and moved to the bungalow there, which he renovated. From here he has run a new combined farm, called Polrose Farm after the names of two of its fields just above Mixtow Pill. He also put up a number of farm sheds at Polrose.

Peter Norman originally trained as an apprentice with English China Clays (when it was English Clays Lovering and Pochin), but he subsequently became a builder. With his brother-in-law, he built seven houses in Blisland and four in Lostwithiel. He now spends much of his time as a builder, employing four men, as well as running Polrose Farm.

The long lane, leading past Castle Farm and reaching to above the River Fowey, now ends at an outlying house. This is Henwood, on the site of an earlier barn and then hunting lodge on land known as Henwood Common. The original small cottage has been extended several times to make a substantial modern house. Its title deeds go back to 1892, when it was sold by Simeon May for £150 to Frederick Tossell, an engineer from Surrey. The Tossell family, whose name in reality seems to have been Bastard, owned Henwood until 1924, when it was sold to Charles Swiggs, a boatman from Bodinnick, for £130. It has passed hands a number of times since then, the longest-term owners being Francis Hayter, an RAF officer, between 1946 and 1966; and the Honourable Sheila Helen Duvollet of Riverhouse, Golant, who owned it between 1966 and 1993. It is currently owned by Miles and Claire Bennett, who live in Birmingham. Its superb location and view over the river have recently been blighted by the building of two wind turbines above the opposite bank of the river, although their erection is currently being challenged in the courts.*

In the lane above Mixtow, running between Castle Farm and Whitecross, a number of new houses have been added to the older ones or have replaced older, smaller houses. The ancient Butter's Tenement was until well after the war the site of a farm labourer's dwelling known as Bunt's Cottage. The freehold of this was sold off by David Oliver to Dave Baker, who owns Southern Cars in Fowey and a car dealership at Hewas Water, west of St Austell. As Windrush Cottage, Dave Baker has considerably increased its size by adding a new back to the house and a separate garage with a flat on top of it. To its north a new cottage, named after the field on which it was built, called Kayes Parc, was built in the 1970s. Percy Ferris moved there when he retired from farming at Lombard. It is currently occupied by David and Dawn Parfitt. (Their son Mark is married to Percy Ferris's daughter, Jane.) On the south side of Windrush Cottage,

---

*   I am very grateful to Claire Bennett for sending me details of the changes of ownership of Henwood, which is sited above an early quay where there was once a ferry. After 1936, when the house was sold by John Swiggs to Nicholas Inch, a butcher from St Austell, the other owners have been Edgar Singer from Newquay (1943–46); Frederick Brown from Barnstaple (1946); David and Deborah Storey from Liskeard (1993–95); and Philip Sharp (1995–96). The Bennetts bought Henwood in 1996. The owners have not usually live there. Madge Norman remembers a man who taught Russian at a Forces language school in Bodmin and his wife there during the Second World War, followed by Hilda Jenkin, whose nerves, shot to pieces in the war, required a very quiet location.

Jill Sprawson, a teacher, lives in a modernised house, Lombard Cottage, once another small cottage.[10]

There are two older houses on the other side of the lane, Restharrow and South Lombard. Restharrow was built in about 1918. Among its owners was Denys Kilham Roberts, a barrister and the long-term Secretary of the Society of Authors, who also edited over twenty-five published collections of poetry and prose. He sold it, shortly before his death in 1976, to Colonel Geoffrey Simpson and his wife, Eileen, both originally from Blackburn, who were looking for a house with a fine view on the coast of the south west to which they could retire after he left the Royal Electrical and Mechanical Engineers. The Simpsons added an extension to the house in 1976–77 and later bought additional land for a second extension from Roy Burrows. The second extension was designed and built by Geoffrey Simpson himself, though its foundations were laid, and the blockwork was carried out, by Peter Norman. The Simpsons moved to live full-time at Restharrow in 1989, after Geoffrey Simpson retired from the army. As they were also very keen sailors, Mixtow Pill offered an excellent base for their 34-foot yacht *Overstretch*, which Geoffrey Simpson had built himself in Germany. Eileen Simpson died in 2011.[11]

South Lombard is on the site of an earlier cottage, but has been extended and modernised. The land it is on was not part of either of the main local estates but belonged in the early years of the nineteenth century to the Reverend John Lewis.[12] Its more recent owners have included Ted Bavin and his wife, Margery (Ted Bavin was, amongst other things, Jeremy Thorpe's accountant; their son was a bishop in South Africa); Air Vice Marshal Peter Williamson, who died in the early 1980s, and his wife, Jill; and Molly Barnaby, the widow of an artist, Tom Barnaby, and the mother of Rosanna Shakerley, the wife of Clive Shakerley, and the grandmother of Justin Shakerley, of Tredudwell; and the sister-in-law of Gavin Shakerley at Hall Farm, Bodinnick. It is currently owned by two psychotherapists, Ilric Shetland and Sally Sales. Ilric Shetland is also a successful artist.*

Stella Poole (1923–2009), who lived at Mixtow House for thirty-two years as a widow after the death of her husband, Bill Poole, in 1976, was

---

* Molly Barnaby could be very difficult. According to her neighbour, Geoffrey Simpson, Molly and Stella Poole 'flew on matching broomsticks'.

a remarkable character. The daughter of a Classics don at Cambridge, she was herself an Oxford History graduate. With dogmatic opinions, in which she was inflexible, and high intelligence, she could at times be very difficult. She was fortunate in having a series of local women of strong character working for her who gave her as good they got. Of these the longest serving was Frieda Collings, followed by Lorraine Sandy until the latter's tragically early death. Stella's last years were made far happier than they would otherwise have been by Hazel Keast, who looked devotedly after Stella's interests at Mixtow, and in Collamere nursing home in Lostwithiel, while also making sure that Stella behaved herself. Stella was however, over the years, an extremely good neighbour to others at Mixtow and a notable presence there. This was more than repaid by her neighbours, Dave and Shirley Bieber at Tonkins Quay House and Linden Blake at Yarkhill.

Following Stella Poole's death, Mixtow House was inherited by her three children. Geoffrey Poole has made a career in IT around the world and currently lives in Hong Kong. Henry Poole has recently retired after forty-three years in the City, specialising in the paper and packaging industry. He is currently writing the life of his grandfather, General Sir Frederick Poole.[*] Lucy Sheppard, whose first career was in the investment side of Barclays Bank in the City, has reinvented herself, following early retirement, as a primary school teacher in Harlesden in north-west London.[†]

After they bought Mixtow House, in 1967, Bill and Stella Poole undertook a substantial renovation programme. Little upkeep, however, was done after Bill's death in 1976. By the time of Stella Poole's death, following several years of ill health, the house required a new roof and a thorough overhaul, carried out over several years. A striking and very successful new addition has been the terrace in front of the house. Filling in the entrance steps leading up to the house on the south side, and levelling the whole area behind it, created a new terrace, five times the size of

---

[*] Sir Frederick and Lady Poole, who lived after the First World War at Torfrey, Golant, are buried in the churchyard at St Sampson's. Their grave has recently been restored by Stella Poole's children.

[†] Geoffrey Poole, who lives with Egidia Wong, has no children. Henry and Diana Poole have three children, Lucy Redman, Antonia Poole and Henry Poole. Lucy and Martin Sheppard, the author of this book, have three children, Catherine Turbett, Eleanor Morrison and Matilda Sheppard.

the old one and connecting the house far more directly to the harbour. The terrace was designed and constructed by Trevor Gynn, the gardener at Mixtow House for many years. Over the last five years, he has also established a fine array of new planting around Mixtow House. This has enhanced the striking views over the harbour from Mixtow House and its garden, reciprocated by the view of Mixtow House itself from the harbour.[*]

One of the most prominent features of Mixtow House, and indeed of Mixtow as a whole, is the rectangular quay in front of it. This dates back to at least the early eighteenth century. Very probably there was a landing place here much earlier than that. It is also clearly shown, with its slipway, on several early naval maps. Used by the US Navy for the repair of landing craft during the Second World War, it was badly damaged by the time of D-Day.[†] Bill and Stella Poole did a considerable amount of work on the quay after they acquired Mixtow House, including restoring the slipway. More recently, major repair and restoration works to the quay, including rebuilding the slipway, have been carried out, directed by Henry Poole.[‡]

---

[*] Trevor Gynn is also the drummer in the popular dance band Silverback, based in Launceston. Hazel Keast, and her husband, Peter, have also done a great deal to help in the restoration and running of Mixtow House.

[†] Mixtow Quay also had a minor role in the 1956 Cold War film, *Doublecross*, in which the villain, the sinister Eastern European Dmitri Krassin, played by Anton Diffring, who has committed murder while stealing secret documents, is seeking to escape by boat to France. To cover his tracks, he ditches his top of the range car at speed off Mixtow Quay. (It would undoubtedly have been seen stranded at the next low tide. It is indeed swiftly recovered in the film.) Directed by Anthony Squire, and starring Donald Houston as a handsome and resourceful local fisherman, the film is set in Fowey and includes several shots of Mixtow. I am very grateful to Dave Bieber for making a copy of this film for me.

[‡] Following the auction of the Mixtow Pill Estate in 1963, there was considerable correspondence between John Carlyon, the new owner of Mixtow House and of the quay, and the other purchasers of parts of the estate as to the exact nature of their respective rights as to the latter's use of the quay. Carlyon acquired a megaphone and used it to tell other people to 'Get off my quay!'. The limitations of the rights of other local householders were clearly defined in counsel's opinion, by A.R. Barrowclough of 3 Pump Court, Temple, dated 24 November 1964. Another ancient right of property-owners was terminated in literally concrete fashion. Worried by the threat of the garden of Portillie slipping onto the path below, Hartley Pollard built a concrete wall narrowing what had once been the only vehicular access to Mixtow House and Dorset Farm.

A spectacular family event, attended by a number of other members of the Mixtow community as well as family and friends, took place on Mixtow Quay on 4 August 2012. A marquee was erected on the quay for the reception following the wedding of Bill and Stella Poole's grand-daughter, Catherine Sheppard, to Garrett Turbett at Lanteglos church. The bride and groom, and many of the guests, landed at the reception from *Moogie*, Dan Hicks's boat, from Polruan. They had arrived at the quay in Polruan in the Polruan Community Bus, driven by John Pollard. The guests later returned by water to where they were staying around the harbour.*

Until recent years, there had always been a few yachts moored in Mixtow Pill in the summer; but there had never been many of them. This has now changed, due to the Fowey Harbour Commission's development of a boat park on the pill. As Fowey is a trust port, run by elected commissioners for the benefit of the port community, the commission has the right to control the area of the harbour above the high-tide mark. For many years, however, it never owned anywhere from which larger boats could be conveniently launched, which inhibited plans to promote Fowey as a yachting centre.

In 2001, however, the commission bought Penmarlam Caravan and Boat Park from David Oliver of Yeate Farm, with the intention of reme-dying this shortcoming. Oliver had built Penmarlam up from modest beginnings. It included a small shop at the top of the hill, above Mixtow Pill, and a launch facility on its banks. These had been linked by a roadway replacing the previous farm track. The commission soon expanded the caravan park to twice its previous size, but then the following year short-sightedly sold it off to defray the cost of its overall purchase. The caravan park was bought by Marcus Wallace, who has since run it as Penmarlam Caravan and Camping Park, with room for sixty-three cara-vans, combined with an enlarged shop.

Both the caravan site and the boat park are called Penmarlam, a name chosen by David Oliver, although its Cornish meaning is unclear.

---

* Another generation connected to Mixtow House, of Stella Poole's grandchil-dren, has now been born: Craig and Eleanor Morrison have a son, Alexander, born on 24 March 2013; Garrett and Catherine Turbett have a daughter, Stella, born 30 September 2013; and Nick and Lucy Redman have a son, Charles, born on 13 June 2014.

It is a pity that the name given to them was not Polmorland or Polmorte, the Cornish name for Mixtow and the name of the fields occupied by Penmarlam. Only the small quay on the southern lip of the pill has retained its historic name, Polmorte Quay. Once dilapidated, it is now a pleasant place to sit. The harbour commission also sold off the old barn or cowshed which had once belonged to Polmorland Farm. It had originally been converted for David Oliver by Richard and Maggie Davies, with a circular staircase built around a ship's mast. A second conversion has recently turned it into a three-bedroom house.

The commission installed enhanced launch facilities and a pontoon reachable at all tides. Penmarlam now attracts many yachts in the summer and is used for storing boats out of the water during the winter. There is also a yacht chandlery and a café, as well as an office, car parks and lavatories. Planning permission was recently granted for expanding the storage facility, in the light of a plan by Imerys to use the upper car park near Caffa Mill, which it owns, for storage to do with its own business. This scheme, however, was put on a backburner, mainly on the grounds of cost, when the present harbour master, Paul Thomas, took over from his predecessor, Tim Jones. The sale of Penmarlam Caravan Park has meant that one obvious area of expansion, for car parking and storage, is unavailable. Recently, it has been announced that the pill will be dredged later this year.*

Penmarlam is not, however, the only nautical presence in or near Mixtow Pill. Above it, between Polmorte Quay and the New Quay, is Lew Roads, the anchorage for a double line of yachts and the overnight mooring of the Bodinnick ferries. A gridiron and mooring rings at Gridiron Beach behind Lew Roads are reminders of the Second World War.[13] There are several skeletons of abandoned boats resting on the pill's beaches, revealed at low water. These include the old ferry (known affectionately as the 'Horse Boat'), which was brought to Mixtow Pill as a pontoon for Kits House Hotel, when it was replaced by a more modern successor. Another may be the ketch *Amanda*, built in Padstow in 1867 and abandoned in the 1930s.[14] A number of the houses on the north bank of Mixtow Pill have also installed their own black plastic pontoons.

Above Mixtow Quay, several older boats in various stages of repair

---

* The harbour commission owns a dredger, the *Lantic Bay*, moored with the tugs. The *Lantic Bay* returned to Fowey, where it worked many years ago, after an overall refit. Information from Dave Baker.

have been long-term fixtures on the beach. These include the *Alice Milford*, belonging to David Luck and with a piano aboard, the *Emma Jane*, the *Kirsten* and the *Petit Mikael*. The harbour commission's tugs have also been a long-term presence opposite Watty's boathouse. Currently, the two tugs are *Cannis* and *Morgawr*. (A third tug, *Cormilan*, went aground on Mundy's Rock leaving Fowey Harbour on 29 April 2014, damaging it beyond viable repair. It was subsequently sold to the Russians, whose safety standards are flexible.) Not all incoming ships now require tugs, but all still have to have a pilot aboard.

It cannot be claimed that Mixtow has had a dramatic impact on the wider world. The history of Mixtow over the years has almost always reflected larger changes in England, Cornwall and Fowey. Farming and fishing are now no longer its main commercial activities, replaced by yachting and holiday letting. Although there is still a core of residents, the majority of whom are retired, many of the houses are second homes or full-time letting properties.

Mixtow, nevertheless, has its own individuality now and has had it over the course of the years, from the heyday of the Mixstowe pirates onwards. Its history provides a portrait of a small, but not insignificant or uninteresting, area over the centuries. Its history also shows what can be discovered about the past life of a small community.

Notes

Notes to Introduction

1   Catherine Parkes, *Fowey Estuary: Historic Audit*, Cornwall Archaeological Unit (Truro, 2000), p. 8.

Notes to Chapter 1

1   For the history of Fowey, see John Keast, *The Story of Fowey* (Redruth, 1950; reprinted 1987), and John Keast, *The Book of Fowey* (Buckingham, 1987); see also, Charles Henderson, *Essays in Cornish History* (Oxford, 1935), pp. 26–43. For the history of Lanteglos, see N.A. Ackland and R.M. Druce, *Lanteglos by Fowey, with Polruan and Bodinnick: The Story of a Parish* (Fowey, 1978; 3rd edition, Lanteglos, 1997).
2   Bodmin Pill was once used by the merchants of Bodmin. Keast, *The Story of Fowey*, p. 15.
3   Keast, *The Story of Fowey*, pp. 2–4; see also, Ackland and Druce, *Lanteglos by Fowey*, p. 4.
4   The industrialist Joseph Treffry planned a suspension bridge, high above the river, as part of a scheme for a road to run between the Torpoint Ferry and St Austell in the 1830s. See John Keast, *'The King of Mid-Cornwall': The Life of Joseph Thomas Treffry (1782–1850)* (Redruth, 1982), pp. 74–81. A 'Design for a Proposed Bridge over the River Fowey' is reproduced, ibid., p. 77. At one point, Treffry's surveyor examined the possibility of a crossing at Mixtow, ibid., p. 78.

5   For Lostwithiel, see Keast, *The Story of Fowey*, pp. 9, 11, 13, 68 and 138. See also, Henderson, *Essays in Cornish History*, pp. 44–53.

6   *The Itinerary of John Leland in or about the Years 1535–1543*, edited by Lucy Toulmin Smith, 5 vols (London, 1907–10), i, pp. 206; 'John Leland, *c.* 1503–1552', *Oxford Dictionary of National Biography*.

7   Lostwithiel, however, retained residual rights to harbour dues until 1869, Helen Doe, *A Maritime History of Fowey Harbour: 'A Fair and Commodious Haven'* (St Agnes, 2010), pp. 5, 6, 30.

8   Tywardreath Priory, a Benedictine house founded by Richard fitz Turold in about 1100 and linked to the monastery of St Sergius and St Bacchus in Angers, held rights over the church and parish of Fowey. Nicholas Orme, *A History of the County of Cornwall*, ii, *Religious History to 1560*, with a Contribution by Oliver Padel, Victoria County History (Woodbridge, 2010), pp. 284–96.

9   It was rededicated in 1336, Pevsner, *Cornwall*, p. 70, but its tower, the second highest in Cornwall, dates from 1460.

10   *The Itinerary of John Leland*, i, p. 203.

11   Fowey was, however, hit hard by the Black Death in the years following 1349. See John Hatcher, *Rural Economy and Society in the Duchy of Cornwall, 1300–1500* (Cambridge, 1970), pp. 120, 142–43, 191. This is the best account of Cornwall's late medieval economy, including agriculture, cloth production, tin mining, fishing and shipping. See ibid., pp. 5, 6, 21, 24, 25, 29–34, 48, 49, 92–94, 120, 169–71, 191, 192, 196, 197, 223–25, 238–45.

12   *The Itinerary of John Leland*, i, p. 203.

13   See Sam Drake, 'Fowey during the Hundred Years' War: A Study of the Port and its People, *c.* 1330 to *c.* 1453', unpublished MA thesis, Royal Holloway University of London, p. 3. I have profited considerably from reading this thesis and discussing medieval Fowey with its author.

14   Keast, *The Story of Fowey*, pp. 10–15, 47–48.

15   See *English Medieval Industries: Craftsmen, Techniques, Products*, ed. John Blair and Nigel Ramsay (London, 2001), pp. 58–62. See also John Hatcher, *English Tin Production and Trade* (Oxford, 1973).

16   Tin production suffered from a severe shortage of labour in the thirty years following the arrival of the Black Death, which increased the price of tin but diminished the quantity produced. Hatcher, *Rural Economy and Society in the Duchy of Cornwall*, pp. 142–43.

17   Drake, 'Fowey during the Hundred Years' War', p. 8.

18   Ackland and Druce, *Lanteglos by Fowey*, pp. 5–6 and 9

19   The witnesses to the release include members of two of the leading families in Fowey, the Mohuns and Treffrys.

20   The feast of St Michael was on 29 September. The date is therefore likely to be 30 September 1409, but it might be 30 September 1410. The regnal years of Henry IV ran from 30 September to 29 September. Rose Boton may have been Rosee Boton.

21   *William Worcestre 'Itineraries': Edited from the Unique MS, Corpus Christi College, Cambridge, 210*, edited by John H. Harvey (Oxford, 1969), pp. 88–91, 96–99, 106–7. The original is in Latin.

22 Both St Saviour's chapel and Lanteglos parish church were held by the hospital of St John at Bridgwater in the early fourteenth century. Keast, *The Story of Fowey*, p. 18.

23 Ackland and Druce, *Lanteglos by Fowey*, pp. 5–6.

24 For an account of St Carroc, see Orme, *A History of the County of Cornwall*, ii, *Religious History to 1560*, pp. 297–99. It is often called St Cadix, but this was a name given it mistakenly in the eighteenth century. St Carroc owned the advowson, the right to appoint the vicar, of the parish church of St Veep, in which St Carroc was situated. St Carroc seems to have been a Welsh saint, an unusual distinction in Cornwall, most of whose saints were either Irish or home-grown. There is now a fine eighteenth-century house, with an earlier core, on the site of St Carroc.

25 *The Itinerary of John Leland*, i, p. 206.

26 Ibid., p. 207. The editor misidentifies 'Poul-morlande' as Penpoll.

27 The name is derived from the common prefix 'pol', for pit or pool, and 'morva', a sea marsh. See O.J. Padel, *Cornish Place-Name Elements*, English Place-Name Society, 56 and 57 (Nottingham, 1985), pp. xxvii, 169. 'Morva' is a far more likely element than 'moyr', blackberries, ibid., p. xxvi. The ending 'land' or 'lande' is an English addition to the Cornish root.

28 Ibid., pp. 84–85. The river's name preceded that of the town.

29 Ackland and Druce, *Lanteglos by Fowey*, pp. 7–8. Later documents refer to another manor, that of Polvethan, which included Polmorland, on the south of Mixtow Pill.

30 Ibid., pp. 9–11.

31 C. Gilbert, *Historical and Topographical Survey of the County of Cornwall*, 2 vols (Plymouth and London, 1817–20), i, p. 897. Gilbert gives the population of the parish as 676 in 1801. Ackland and Druce, *Lanteglos by Fowey*, p. 8.

32 Catherine Parkes, *Fowey Estuary: Historic Audit*, Cornwall Archaeological Unit (Truro, 2000), p. 41.

33 *Richard Carew of Antony: The Survey of Cornwall &*, edited with an introduction by F.E. Halliday (London, 1953), pp. 81–237.

34 Ackland and Druce, *Lanteglos by Fowey*, p. 22.

35 *Richard Carew of Antony: The Survey of Cornwall*, p. 102.

36 Ackland and Druce, *Lanteglos by Fowey*, p. 12. Botters left his four sons and three daughters one sheep each.

37 See *Richard Carew of Antony: The Survey of Cornwall*, pp. 117–19, for Cornish pilchard fishing. Carew was exceptionally knowledgeable about fishing and gives a detailed account of what fish were caught and the methods used to take and process them. See also, Keast, *The Book of Fowey*, pp. 39–42.

38 *Richard Carew of Antony: The Survey of Cornwall*, p. 206.

39 Ackland and Druce, *Lanteglos by Fowey*, p. 13.

40 Ibid., p. 13.

41 Richard Williams, *Limekilns and Limeburning* (Aylesbury, 1989).

42 Ackland and Druce, *Lanteglos by Fowey*, p. 13. The drawing is in Cornwall Record Office, DDF 327/13.

43 For the variants on the name, see above, p. 6n.

44 Keast, *The Story of Fowey*, p. 21.

45 Ibid., pp. 14, 15, 18, 19, 25, 27–30. The Mixtowes' house may indeed have been on the site of Place.

46 I owe this important point to Sam Drake.

47 Keast, *The Story of Fowey*, pp. 24–33; Keast, *The Book of Fowey*, pp. 17–20. For Fowey's, and Mixtow's, piratical history, see C.L. Kingsford, 'West Country Piracy: The School of English Seamen', in *Prejudice and Promise in Fifteenth-Century England* (1925; reprinted, London, 1962), pp. 78–106, plus appendix, pp. 179–203. See also *A Calendar of Early Chancery Proceedings Relating to West Country Shipping, 1388–1493*, edited with an Introduction by Dorothy M. Gardiner, Devon and Cornwall Record Society, new series, vol. 21, pp. vii-xix, 9–13, 21–23, 28, 31–33, 36, 37, 44, 54, 55, 59, 60, 65–67, 69–71, 78, 79, 81–83, 90–92, 97, 102–4, 114–19.

48 Keast, *The Story of Fowey*, pp. 24–25. The chain may, in fact, have antedated the French raid.

49 It is impossible to trace the exact relationship between the Mixstowes or Michelstowes of different generations. See, however, the forthcoming entry on the family by Sam Drake in the *Oxford Dictionary of National Biography*.

50 *Calendar of Patent Rolls, 1345–48*, pp. 115–16. I am most grateful to Sam Drake for drawing this reference to my attention.

51 Keast, *The Story of Fowey*, p. 28.

52 *Calendar of Patent Rolls, 1391–96*, 9 May 1393, p. 263.

53 *A Calendar of Early Chancery Proceedings Relating to West Country Shipping*, no. 26, p. 28. Brittany, at the time, was not part of France, being ruled by a duke.

54 Ibid., pp. 25–30.

55 *Richard Carew of Antony: The Survey of Cornwall*, p. 210; Keast, *The Story of Fowey*, pp. 32–33; Gilbert, *Historical and Topographical Survey of the County of Cornwall*, i, p. 14. For the acquisition of the name 'Fowey Gallants', see *The Itinerary of John Leland*, i, pp. 203–4: 'The shippes of Fawy sayling by Rhie and Winchelsey about Edward the 3. tyme wold vale no bonet being requirid, wherapon Rhy and Winchelsey men and they faught, wher Fawey men had victorie, and thereupon bare their armes with the armes of Rhy and Winchelsey: and then rose the name of the Gallaunts of Fowey'.

56 A.L. Rowse, *Tudor Cornwall* (London, 1941), pp. 38–81.

57 See the entries for Fowey in *The History of Parliament: The House of Commons* between 1558 and 1832.

58 Keast, *The Story of Fowey*, p. 21.

59 Ibid., pp. 45–46.

60 Mary Coate, *Cornwall in the Great Civil War and Interregnum, 1642–1660* (Truro, 1963), pp. 131–63; Keast, *The Story of Fowey*, pp. 59–63. The Parliamentary cavalry, however, broke out and escaped to Plymouth.

61 Keast, *The Story of Fowey*, pp. 60–61; *Diary of Richard Symonds*, Camden Society (1859). Listithiel is of course Lostwithiel and Glant is Golant. Carew gives a famous description of Hall Walk in his survey, *Richard Carew of Antony: The Survey of Cornwall*, p. 206.

62 Keast, *The Story of Fowey*, p. 61. Fowey was notable in this period for having produced one of the men most hated by Royalists: Oliver Cromwell's chaplain Hugh Peters, a cousin of John Treffry, the owner of Place. Although he had not signed the king's death warrant, Peters was excluded from the pardon offered by Charles II on his Restoration in 1660. After being captured and tried, he was executed at Charing Cross in October 1660. For Peters, see ibid., pp. 58, 64, 65, 144, 157–58; and 'Hugh Peters (1598–1660)', *Oxford Dictionary of National Biography*.

63 Victor Stater, *Duke Hamilton is Dead! A Story of Aristocratic Life and Death in Stuart Britain* (New York, 1999), pp. 203–38, 279.

64 For Pitt, see 'Thomas Pitt (1653–1726)', *Oxford Dictionary of National Biography*.

65 British Library, Cotton MS Augustus I, i, 35, 36, 38, 39. This has been described as 'the largest single British government mapping initiative before the nineteenth century', *Henry VIII: Man and Monarch* (British Library Exhibition Catalogue, London, 2009), p. 216. For a later reproduction of this map, see Keast, *The Story of Fowey*, p. 40.

66 A.H.W. Robinson, *Marine Cartography in Britain* (London, 1962), pp. 105–11.

67 These charts, and many successors, can best be seen at the National Hydrographic Office, Taunton.

68 For Wiseman's stone, see Parkes, *Fowey Estuary*, p. 42. I have discovered no information about the lepers said to have lived there.

69 Parkes, *Fowey Estuary*, pp. 12, 16, 38 and 80.

70 Ibid., p. 42.

Notes to Chapter 2

1 Cornwall Record Office, F/327/12.

2 *Royal Cornwall Gazette*, 26 June 1814.

3 Three copies were made: one for the parish, one for the diocese and one for the government. The last of these is now in the National Archives: see National Archives, IR 29/6/102 and IR 30/6/102.

4 National Archives, IR 18 /437, report on the completion of the tithe redemption agreement, 8 August 1845.

5 The road directly up to White Cross (or Whitacross, but contracted to Whitecross in modern times) from the ferry landing dates from the second half of the nineteenth century.

6 Information from Nick Hill, National Conservation Projects Manager, National Trust, Exmoor.

7 Officially Grade 2: 'House circa 1830s with circa mid C18 parallel wing to rear comprising cottage. Rubble stone with whitewashed slate hung south front. Hipped roof with hipped end to read projecting wing and gabled ends to rear cottage. L-shaped plan with cottage at angle running parallel to main front. 2 storeys. South front, symmetrical 3 window front. Ground floor with two 24 pane

sashes without horns flanking glazed central door with doorcase with moulded entablature and flanking pilasters. Intersecting glazing bars in fanlight above'.

8   Cornwall Record Office, R/1883. The final figure in the 1590s date is difficult to make out; it is probably 1592.

9   Cornwall Record Office, R/1971.

10 John Couch was almost certainly related to Sir Arthur Quiller-Couch, who was born Arthur Couch and whose family originated in Polperro, in the parish of Talland.

11 Cornwall Record Office, R/1682. The lease reserved mineral and timber rights to the freeholder. I have added punctuation.

12 Cornwall Record Office, R/5304/30.

13 Richard Salt was the great great great grandfather of Dr Helen Doe, the maritime historian who now lives at Penolva in Mixtow. The limekiln used land belonging to Mixtow House and Tonkin's Quay.

14 Three belonging to Rosebank and two to the representatives of Peter Tonkin.

15 Cornwall Record Office, R/1678–82. The manor of Polvethan is not mentioned in early deeds about Lanteglos.

16 *Royal Cornwall Gazette*, 29 December 1832.

17 Ibid.

18 C.H. Ward-Jackson, *Ships and Shipbuilders of a Westcountry Port: Fowey, 1796–1939* (Truro, 1986), pp. 5–62.

19 *Royal Cornwall Gazette*, 15 March 1844.

20 *Royal Cornwall Gazette*, 12 June 1846.

21 *Royal Cornwall Gazette*, 28 June 1861; the advertisement was repeated on 5 and 12 July 1861.

22 Cornwall Record Office, DD, GRA 85.

23 A Worcester businessman, Alexander Clunes Sheriff (1816–1878) was Liberal MP for Worcester from 1865 to 1878. He was the brother-in-law rather than the brother of Thomas Clunes senior.

24 *Royal Cornwall Gazette*, 17 October 1879.

25 *Berrow's Worcester Journal*, 15 March 1879. Kelly's directory for 1878 shows Clunes living at Mixtow.

26 *Royal Cornwall Gazette*, 14 August 1885.

27 *Royal Cornwall Gazette*, 15 September 1898.

28 As there were numerous medieval and post-medieval quays along the river, there must have been a landing place at Mixtow in earlier times, but its exact location is unclear. See Catherine Parkes, *Fowey Estuary: Historic Audit*, Cornwall Archaeological Unit (Truro, 2000), p. 18.

29 *London Evening Post*, 21 September 1797.

30 Cornwall Record Office, R/1970. See also, R/1673–75.

31 The limekiln shown on the Boconnoc Estate terrier, Cornwall Record Office, F/327/12, of 1814 was on the site of what then became a boathouse and is now Tonkins Quay House. When the river wall of the house collapsed in 2002, under-pinning works revealed the remains of a limekiln. Information from Dave Bieber.

32 Cornwall Record Office, DDR (5) 1/770, 23 December 1818.

33 National Archives, IR 29/6/102 and IR 30/6/102.

34 Cornwall Record Office, DDF (4), 160/1. See also, CF/1/1590.

35 Cornwall Record Office, AP/K/763.

36 *Cornwall Royal Gazette*, 16 April 1814. The exact terms of the will are difficult to follow. Knight, the Willcocks and Thomas Nichols seem, however, to have been related.

37 *Cornwall Royal Gazette*, 4 June 1814.

38 Chart of Fowey Harbour, 1813, National Hydrographic Office.

39 *The Memoirs of Susan Sibbald (1783–1812)*, edited by Francis Paget Hett (London, 1926). Susan Mein married Colonel William Sibbald of the 15th Regiment of Foot and, after his death, moved to Canada. Her mother was Margaret Ellis of Orchard and Grove, Cornwall.

40 *The Memoirs of Susan Sibbald*, p. 171.

41 Ibid., pp. 24, 175.

42 Ibid., p. 173.

43 *Royal Cornwall Gazette*, 28 April 1843; Ward-Jackson, *Ships and Shipbuilders of a Westcountry Port*, pp. 42–43. The *Royal Adelaide* specialised in carrying emigrants to Quebec.

44 *Royal Cornish Gazette*, 18 May 1849.

45 *Royal Cornwall Gazette*, 11 April 1856.

46 Henry Vulliamy left his wife his estate, including Rosebank, in his will, dated 26 November 1890.

47 For Atkinson, Alison Prince, *Kenneth Grahame: An Innocent in the Wild Wood* (London, 1994), pp. 163, 178, 201–3,222, 236, 242, 247, 249, 251, 263, 267–68; Joan Coombs, *A Fowey Jig-Saw: The History of the Royal Fowey Yacht Club* (Fowey, 2000), pp. 34–36, 44, 54–56, 65, 80, 86–87, 137, 171 and 175.

48 'Sir Arthur Thomas Quiller-Couch (1863–1944)', *Oxford Dictionary of National Biography*; Prince, *Kenneth Grahame*, pp. 162–67, 171–72, 188, 204, 242, 247–49, 260, 262–63.

49 Coombs, *A Fowey Jig-Saw*, pp. 91–114.

50 Prince, *Kenneth Grahame*, pp. 215–40; Kenneth Grahame, *My Dearest Mouse: The 'Wind in the Willows' Letters*, introduction by David Gooderson (London, 1988); 'Kenneth Grahame (1859–1932)', *Oxford Dictionary of National Biography*.

51 All the following details can be found in the National Archives, IR 58/71785, with corresponding maps in IR 128/5/628 and 632. The valuations were completed between 1910 and 1915. The returns also provide details of tithe and land tax rates, rights of way, liabilities for insurance and repair, and sporting rights (worth £75 at Yeate and £25 at Castle).

52 In 1841, Castle had been occupied and farmed by John Glanville and his wife Ann. Their eight children, as well as an agricultural labourer, were living in the house.

53 Coombs, *A Fowey Jig-Saw*, pp. 86–90, for a full account of the tragedy. Prince, *Kenneth Grahame*, pp. 267–68, gives an inaccurate version of the events.

54 Kenneth Grahame to Austin Purves, 20 September 1911, quoted in Prince, *Kenneth Grahame*, p. 268.

55 Ibid., p. 274.
56 Edward Atkinson, will, 9 October 1909; probate to Kate Isabel Marston, sole executrix, 27 December 1911.
57 An agreement between J.C.S. Rashleigh and Mrs A.M. Rainey, dated 10 December 1915, assured the latter's rights to a share of the water arising from a spring at Dorset Farm. This was the outcome of a legal action, *Rainey* v. *Lamb*, 1913, R. no. 1174, in the Chancery Division of the High Court. William Lamb was the tenant of Dorset Farm.
58 Royal Institution of Cornwall, F/3/2/27, dated 15 September 1915. The land was still occupied by Herbert Carnall in 1932.
59 Information on Archie Watty and the King family from Richard and Simon King.
60 Information from Richard and Simon King.
61 Alice Mary Rainey, will, dated 7 March 1927. Her address at that time was 77 Park Lane, Croydon, but she died at 10 Kensington Crescent, Kensington, on 11 November 1930. She left instructions that she was to be buried in the grave of her second husband. She left £21,962 8s. 3d.

Notes to Chapter 3

1 Captain Nicholas Eveleigh, the tenant of Mixtow House in 1832, was also probably a naval officer.
2 John Keast, *The Story of Fowey* (Redruth, 1950; reprinted 1987), pp. 121–22, 124. The First World War memorial at Lanteglos church lists twenty-three men from the parish killed in the war. Of these eight were sailors. The memorial at Fowey includes men killed at Coronel and Jutland, and in Mesopotamia.
3 R.M. Barton, *A History of the China-Clay Industry* (Truro, 1966), pp. 152, 154, 162, 164.
4 F.E. Halliday, *A History of Cornwall* (London, 1959), pp. 307–8.
5 For Fowey between 1939 and 1945, see *Never Forget: Fowey Remembers. Fiftieth Anniversary of D-Day 1994* (Fowey, 1994), and Paul Richards and Derek Reynolds, *Fowey at War* (Fowey, 1994). For the RAF contribution, see Alexander Hurn, *Royal Air Force: Fowey* (Cardiff, 1993); and Richards and Reynolds, *Fowey at War*, pp. 25–27. Unfortunately, none of these publications provide notes on their sources.
6 For these defences, see Richards and Reynolds, *Fowey at War*, pp. 8–9.
7 Fowey and Mixtow also took its share of evacuees. According to Olive Motton, an evacuee family of four lived in Mixtow Farm's barn. There were evacuees also at South Lombards. In addition, a number of Land Army girls worked on the farms in Mixtow, including for a time Daphne Du Maurier's sister, Angela.
8 For a list of the requisitioned buildings, see Richards and Reynolds, *Fowey at War*, pp. 25–26. See also, ibid., pp. 34–35, for the strength of Army units stationed at Fowey and for the local Home Guard.

9   Fowey Harbour Commssioners, log book, 25 March, 23 April, 28 May, 25 June and 23 July 1941. I am grateful to Paul Richards for these references.

10 See Richards and Reynolds, *Fowey at War*, pp. 10–14.

11 It was on the site of what is now the main car park in Polruan.

12 For these attacks, see Richards and Reynolds, *Fowey at War*, pp. 3–4. Madge Norman remembers the German planes' unnerving habit of hedge-hopping and one raid when the air raid warnings only went off after the raid itself was over.

13 Although some china clay was shipped out during the war from the docks, the tonnage fell to a fraction of the level of 1939. From 468,278 tons shipped in 1939, the quantity fell to 35,244 tons in 1942. Richards and Reynolds, *Fowey at War*, p. 37.

14 *Royal Air Force: Fowey*, p. 8.

15 The original forms are at the National Archives. For Lanteglos see MAF 32 421/1. The corresponding maps, coloured in on 1907 Ordnance Survey maps and showing individual holdings, are in MAF 73 7/52.

16 The Boconnoc Estate owned Dorset, Lombard and Yeate. Miss Lamb, of Roseview, Lostwithiel, owned Castle Farm. Mixtow Farm was owned by Robert Varco of Fowey.

17 William Tapley had acquired Mixtow House from Robert Varco in 1940. The MAF return of the same year shows that he was already in residence.

18 Richards and Reynolds, *Fowey at War*, pp. 38–39; *Never Forget*, pp. 25–29.

19 *Never Forget*, p. 27.

20 Ibid., p. 15.

21 See Richards and Reynolds, *Fowey at War*, pp. 41–42; and *Never Forget*, pp. 21 and 34.

22 Probably Maintenance Operations Management.

23 This was clearly the house originally called Rose Hill and now called Rosebank.

24 Memories of Robert Bond, ex-US Navy, who revisited Mixtow in the 1970s.

25 *Never Forget*, p. 21. The Americans also managed to overturn a truck on one occasion, on the way back from a convivial evening at the Punchbowl at Lanreath. Information from Frank and Madge Norman.

26 Information from Lorna Tubb.

27 This track and gun-site are now overgrown but still possible to identify.

28 *Never Forget*, p. 22.

29 Ibid., p. 4.

30 For the complicated manoeuvres involved, see *Never Forget*, pp. 30–32. For a list of landing craft based at Fowey, Richards and Reynolds, *Fowey at War*, pp. 45–47.

31 *Never Forget*, p. 18.

32 Richards and Reynolds, *Fowey at War*, pp. 45, 47–48.

33 *Never Forget*, p. 21.

Notes to Chapter 4

1   Journal by an Oxford man, possibly J. Forsyth, 1759, *Devon and Cornwall Notes and Queries*, 23 (1947–49), p. 281.

2   For a well-researched account of ship-building in Fowey, which reflected the changing demands of trade, see C.H. Ward-Jackson, *Ships and Shipbuilders of a Westcountry Seaport: Fowey, 1796–1939* (Truro, 1986), pp. 5–62. For the smuggling, and the ships built for it, ibid., pp. 5–21. As Fowey was the centre of the anti-smuggling operations of the Revenue officers, contraband was usually landed away from the town itself.

3   For the history of the china clay industry, see R.M. Barton, *A History of the China-Clay Industry* (Truro, 1966); and Kenneth Hudson, *The History of English China Clays: Fifty Years of Pioneering and Growth* (Newton Abbot, 1969). I am most grateful to Ivor Bowditch and Derek Giles, of the China Clay History Society, for telling me about the history of English China Clays. A number of the main documents to do with the redevelopment of the docks at the end of the 1960s are to be found in the National Archives, DK 1/274.

4   Barton, *A History of the China-Clay Industry*, p. 75. Treffry's initial concern was to ship granite from his quarries and copper from his Fowey Consols mine. Treffry, the nephew and heir of William Treffry of Place, was born Joseph Thomas Austen, but changed his name to Treffry in 1836. He was involved in many other industrial enterprises, including railways, road-making and shipping, and also built the harbour at Newquay. See John Keast, *'The King of Mid-Cornwall': The Life of Joseph Thomas Treffry (1782–1850)* (Redruth, 1982).

5   Barton, *A History of the China-Clay Industry*, p. 75. For Treffry's activities at Caffa Mill, Keast, *'The King of Mid-Cornwall'*, pp. 9, 45–49.

6   Barton, *A History of the China-Clay Industry*, pp. 75–76.

7   Jim Lewis, *A Richly Yielding Piece of Ground: The Story of Fowey Consols Mine Near St Blazey* (St Austell, 1997), pp. 28–31. I am grateful to Dr Helen Doe for drawing this book to my attention.

8   Barton, *A History of the China-Clay Industry*, p. 76; Keast, *'The King of Mid-Cornwall'*, pp. 55–72. Par was formed at the mouth of a small river, the Luxulyan.

9   Hudson, *The History of English China Clays*, p. 137. See, however, John Keast, *'The King of Mid-Cornwall'*, pp. 74–81, for a plan to build a bridge.

10 John Stengelhofen, *Cornwall's Railway Heritage* (revised edn, Truro, 2003), pp. 15–19.

11 Barton, *A History of the China-Clay Industry*, pp. 131–32; Keast, *The Story of Fowey*, p. 108. The Cornwall Minerals Railway was assured considerable traffic by its associate, the Cornwall Consolidated Iron Mines Corporation, though its highly ambitious plans for iron ore shipment failed to materialise.

12 Barton, *A History of the China-Clay Industry*, p. 132.

13 For details of the two railways, see Colin and David McCarthy, *Railways of Britain: Devon and Cornwall* (London, 2008), pp. 42–53. See also Stengelhofen, *Cornwall's Railway Heritage*, pp. 15–20, 23.

14 Hudson, *The History of English China Clays*, p. 58. The first three jetties were built to ship iron ore, the others to ship china clay. Iron ore shipments declined in the last quarter of the nineteenth century.

15 The three original constituent companies were Martin Brothers Ltd, the West of England and Great Beam Co. Ltd, and the North Cornwall China Clay Co. Ltd. See Barton, *A History of the China-Clay Industry*, p. 165. English China Clays became one of the original hundred companies when the FTSE index was established in 1984.

16 Hudson, *The History of English China Clays*, pp. 137–38.

17 English Clays Lovering Pochin and Co., 'Notes of the Intended Development of Fowey Jetties', 11 September 1967, pp. 1–2.

18 In 1967 Nos 3 and 4 Jetties at Fowey were handling 500,000 tons a year, while No. 8 was handling 250,000 tons.

19 Part of the harbour improvement plan included a major dredging programme and the removal of the Carne Rock, an underwater hazard.

20 English Clays Lovering Pochin and Co., 'Notes of the Intended Development of Fowey Jetties', 11 September 1967.

21 English Clays Lovering Pochin and Co., 'Notes of the Intended Development of Fowey Jetties', 11 September 1967, p. 6, 'Anticipated Effects of the Proposed Development'.

22 *Cornish Times*, 8 September 1967. For local reaction, ibid., 5 May; 8, 15 and 22 September; 13 October; and 3 and 17 November 1967.

23 *Cornish Times*, 22 September 1967.

24 National Trust leaflet, 'Coast of Cornwall' (no date), p. 9. I am grateful to Andy Simmons of the National Trust for sending me a copy of this leaflet.

25 Alan Dalton to Barbara Castle MP, 14 February 1968. He later became Sir Alan Dalton CBE.

26 An extensive archive of photograph, showing the stages and details of construction, is held at the China Clay History Society's archives. The China Clay History Society is part of the Wheal Martyn Trust, Carthew, St Austell PL26 8XG.

Notes to Chapter 5

1 Information about the King family from Richard and Simon King.

2 Priscilla Smart died in 2000. Arthur Smart, whose mother was Japanese, died in 2014.

3 Diana Allden died in 2011.

4 Paul Tuck, a chartered accountant, lectures on accounting at Buckingham University. Penny Tuck is Professor of Accounting, Public Finance and Policy at the University of Birmingham.

5 Kits House Hotel brochure. I am grateful to Dr Sheila Cheadle for giving me a copy of this.

6 Information about Walter Olding from Madge Norman and Hilary Severn.

7   Information from Frank and Madge Norman.

8   Information on these farms from Iain and Madge Norman.

9   Information from Dave and Catherine Collins.

10   Information from Dave Baker and from David and Dawn Parfitt.

11   Information from Geoffrey Simpson. Jimmy Holten, a Bodinnick ferryman, had lived at Restharrow before Kilham Roberts.

12   Cornwall Record Office, DDF, 327/13. According to this Boconnoc terrier, the Reverend Lewis had recently died. Two other nearby fields belonged to Mrs J. Lewis.

13   Catherine Parkes, *Fowey Estuary: Historic Audit*, Cornwall Archaeological Unit (Truro, 2000), p. 19. There is also a mooring ring on the beach just above Mixtow Quay.

14   Ibid., pp. 22, 42.

Bibliography

Archives

British Library

Cotton MS Augustus I, i, 35, 36, 38, 39
Newspapers, *Berrow's Worcester Journal; Cornish Times; London Evening Post; Royal Cornwall Gazette.*

China Clay History Society

English Clays Lovering Pochin and Co., 'Notes on the Intended Development of Fowey Jetties', 11 September 1967.
Rendel, Palmer and Tritton, 'Report on the Development of the Port of Fowey', July 1967.
Letter, Alan Dalton to Barbara Castle MP, 14 February 1968.

Cornwall Record Office

DD, GRA 85   Mixtow inventory, 19 March 1878
DDF, (4), 160/1   Merrifield lease, 1727

DDR (5), 1/770   Mixtow letter, 23 December 1818
F/1/327/12   Boconnoc Estate terrier, 1814
R/1673–82   Mixtow leases
R/1965–75   Mixtow leases

National Archives

ADM 1/13198   Correspondence on landing craft repair
DK 1/274   Dock redevelopment, Fowey and Parr
IR 18/437   Tithe Redemption, Lanteglos by Fowey, summary
IR 29/6/102   Tithe Redemption, Lanteglos by Fowey, map
IR 30/6/102   Tithe Redemption, Lanteglos by Fowey, list
IR 58/71785   Land Tax, Lanteglos by Fowey, list
IR 128/5/628   Land Tax, Lanteglos by Fowey, map
IR 128/5/632   Land Tax, Lanteglos by Fowey, map
MAF 32 421/1   Farm Survey, Lanteglos by Fowey, survey
MAF 73 7/52   Farm Survey, Lanteglos by Fowey, map

Royal Institution of Cornwall, Courtney Library, Truro

F/3/2/27   Sale, Polmorland, 15 September 1915
TAM/1/3/32/3   Release, Mixtow, 30 September 1430

Other Sources

Auction Catalogue, Mixtow Pill Estate, May, Whetter & Grose, 1 April 1963.

Censuses: 1841, 1851, 1861, 1871, 1881, 1891, 1901, 1911.

Interviews: Jonathan Allden; Frank and Sue Ashworth; Dave Baker; Miles Bennett; Tony Berkeley; Dave and Shirley Bieber; Linden Blake; Lyn Carter; Sheila Cheadle; Dave and Catherine Collins; Murray and Gloria Collings; Angela and Les Couch; Keverne Crapp; Richard and Maggie Davies; Tony and Betty Davies; Helen Doe; Colin Ferris; Christina and Richard Geering; Paul and Janet Harvey; Richard and Simon King;

Frank and Madge Norman; Iain Norman; David and Dawn Parfitt; Jane Parfitt; Isabel Pickering; John and Ginny Pollard; Henry and Geoffrey Poole; Sally Sales; Vivian Sandy; Robert Saxton; George Seppings; Hilary Severn; Lucy Sheppard; Geoffrey Simpson; Lorna Tubb; Paul and Penelope Tuck; Marcus Wallace; Naomi Wilmot.

Wills: Edward Atkinson, 9 October 1909; Alice Mary Rainey, 7 March 1927; William Tapley, 14 December 1952; Robert Varco, 18 December 1953.

Books

N.A. Ackland and R.M. Druce, *Lanteglos by Fowey, with Polruan and Bodinnick: The Story of a Parish* (Fowey, 1978; 3rd edition, Lanteglos, 1997).

Arthur Baker, *Royal Air Force, Fowey: A History of 1101 Marine Craft Unit* (n.p., 1993).

R.M. Barton, *A History of the China-Clay Industry* (Truro, 1966).

John Blair and Nigel Ramsay, ed., *English Medieval Industries: Craftsmen, Techniques, Products* (London, 2001).

Richard Carew, *Richard Carew of Antony: The Survey of Cornwall &*, edited with an introduction by F.E. Halliday (London, 1953).

Mary Coate, *Cornwall in the Great Civil War and Interregnum, 1642–1660* (Truro, 1963).

Joan Coombs, *A Fowey Jig-Saw: The History of the Royal Fowey Yacht Club* (Fowey, 2000).

Helen Doe, *A Maritime History of Fowey Harbour: 'A Fair and Commodious Haven'* (St Agnes, 2010).

Sam Drake, 'Fowey during the Hundred Years' War: A Study of the Port and its People, *c.* 1330 to *c.* 1453', unpublished MA thesis, Royal Holloway University of London.

Dorothy M. Gardiner, ed., *A Calendar of Early Chancery Proceedings Relating to West Country Shipping, 1388–1493*, Devon and Cornwall Record Society, new series, vol. 2.

C. Gilbert, *Historical and Topographical Survey of the County of Cornwall*, 2 vols (Plymouth and London, 1817–20).

Kenneth Grahame, *My Dearest Mouse: The 'Wind in the Willows' Letters*, introduction by David Gooderson (London, 1988).

F.E. Halliday, *A History of Cornwall* (London, 1959).

John H. Harvey , ed., *William Worcestre 'Itineraries': Edited from the Unique MS, Corpus Christi College, Cambridge, 210* (Oxford, 1969).

Henry VIII: Man and Monarch (British Library Exhibition Catalogue, London, 2009).

John Hatcher, *English Tin Production and Trade* (Oxford, 1973).

John Hatcher, *Rural Economy and Society in the Duchy of Cornwall, 1300–1500* (Cambridge, 1970).

Charles Henderson, *Essays in Cornish History* (Oxford, 1935).

Kenneth Hudson, *The History of English China Clays: Fifty Years of Pioneering and Growth* (Newton Abbot, 1969).

Alexander Hurn, *Royal Air Force: Fowey* (Cardiff, 1993).

John Keast, *The Book of Fowey* (Buckingham, 1987).

John Keast, *'The King of Mid-Cornwall': The Life of Joseph Thomas Treffry (1782–1850)* (Redruth, 1982).

John Keast, *The Story of Fowey* (Redruth, 1950; reprinted 1987).

C.L. Kingsford, 'West Country Piracy: The School of English Seamen', in *Prejudice and Promise in Fifteenth-Century England* (1925; reprinted, London, 1962).

John Leland, *The Itinerary of John Leland in or about the Years 1535–1543*, edited by Lucy Toulmin Smith, 5 vols (London, 1907–10).

Jim Lewis, *A Richly Yielding Piece of Ground: The Story of Fowey Consols Mine Near St Blazey* (St Austell, 1997).

Colin and David McCarthy, *Railways of Britain: Devon and Cornwall* (London, 2008)

John Morris, ed., *Domesday Book: Cornwall* (Chichester, 1979).

National Trust, leaflet, 'Coast of Cornwall' (no date).

Never Forget: Fowey Remembers. Fiftieth Anniversary of D-Day 1994 (Fowey, 1994).

Nicholas Orme, *A History of the County of Cornwall*, ii, *Religious History to 1560*, with a Contribution by Oliver Padel, Victoria County History (Woodbridge, 2010).

Oxford Dictionary of National Biography, 'Kenneth Grahame, 1859–1932'; 'John Leland, c. 1503–1552'; 'Hugh Peters, 1598–1660'; 'Thomas Pitt, 1653–1726'; 'Sir Arthur Thomas Quiller-Couch, 1863–1944'.

O.J. Padel, *A Popular Dictionary of Cornish Place-Names* (Penzance, 1988).

O.J. Padel, *Cornish Place-Name Elements*, English Place-Name Society, 56 and 57 (Nottingham, 1985).

Catherine Parkes, *Fowey Estuary Historic Audit* (Cornwall Archaeological Unit, 2000).

Nikolaus Pevsner, *Cornwall* (second edn, Harmondsworth, 1970).

Isabel Pickering, *Some Goings On! A Selection of Newspaper Articles about Fowey, Polruan and Lanteglos from 1800–1899* (Fowey, 1995).

Alison Prince, *Kenneth Grahame: An Innocent in the Wild Wood* (London, 1994).

Arthur Quiller-Couch, *The Astonishing History of Troy Town* (1888).

Paul Richards and Derek Reynolds, *Fowey at War* (Fowey, 1994).

A.H.W. Robinson, *Marine Cartography in Britain* (London, 1962).

A.L. Rowse, *Tudor Cornwall* (London, 1941).

Susan Sibbald, *The Memoirs of Susan Sibbald (1783–1812)*, edited by Francis Paget Hett (London, 1926).

Victor Stater, *Duke Hamilton is Dead! A Story of Aristocratic Life and Death in Stuart Britain* (New York, 1999).

John Stengelhofen, *Cornwall's Railway Heritage* (revised edn, Truro, 2003).

Richard Symonds, *Diary of Richard Symonds*, Camden Society (1859).

Index

All place-names are in Cornwall, unless stated otherwise.